Count...

Countdown Puzzle Book

By Michael Wylie and Damian Eadie

Preface by Richard Whiteley

GRANADA

Countdown is the creation of Armond Jammot;
it is a Yorkshire Television production

First published in Great Britain in 2001
by Granada Media, an imprint of André Deutsch Limited
20 Mortimer Street
London W1T 3JW

In association with Granada Media Group

A catalogue record for this book is available from the British Library

ISBN 0 233 99943 4

Photography by Granada Media
Cover design by Slatter Anderson

Typeset by Derek Doyle & Associates, Liverpool
Printed and bound in the UK by
Mackays of Chatham plc, Chatham, Kent, UK

10 9 8 7 6 5 4 3 2 1

Contents

Contents

Foreword

by Richard Whiteley

Hello and welcome to this monster book of *Countdown* brainteasers. What a delight! Here are pages and pages of words and number games for you to indulge in to your heart's content.

This is a good old-fashioned puzzle book. Just like the television programme, there are no gimmicks or gizmos here – we're a computer free zone! All the games have been painstakingly worked out by Michael Wylie and Damian Eadie. Both (of course) are producers of *Countdown* and both former finalists – Michael way back in 1983, where he lost to Joyce Cansfield in Series 1, and Damian, a positive new boy, who triumphed in the final of Series 28 over Wayne Kelly in 1994.

People often call *Countdown* a quiz show but, in the strictest sense, it is not. There are no questions, merely a set of problems which require solutions. I like to call it a parlour game, in the great tradition of the programmes which were on the wireless when I was a child. Do you remember *Twenty Questions*? You had to guess an object with the help of just three clues – animal, vegetable or mineral. Or how about *Have a Go*, in which Wilfred Pickles and Mabel interviewed people in village halls all over the country? These programmes ran for years and millions tuned in.

The same can be said of television. We got a television set in 1952 (well before the Coronation which made us very posh!) and one of my earliest recollections is of tuning into *What's My Line*. A panel of four had to guess someone's job, helped only by a simple mime act. The programme ran for years in Britain and it is still broadcast in many places all over the world. All of these programmes – all based on simple concepts – have stood the test of time. And so, I think, has *Countdown*. It retains its original look (a look we thought was trendy in 1982 but now seems positively retro) and that is the beauty of it. We won't change anything just for the sake of it. We believe that is why many millions find the programme so addictive. And because we will never run out of words or numbers – there is no reason why *Countdown* shouldn't continue to run and run.

When we started out in November 1982, as the first programme on Channel 4's opening night, we had been given a five-week run. Who would have believed then that we would go on to clock up over 18 years and 3,000 programmes? In 2001 we are still going strong, with over 3.5 million viewers each day and a contract from Channel 4 until mid-2004!

For so many of us – young and old – *Countdown* at 4.30 in the afternoon has established itself as a fixed point in our daily timetable. It's an all too brief but reliable period in which to forget the hurly burly outside and exercise our brains. For every Granny and Granddad watching there is a grandson and granddaughter, which means we are constantly replenishing our audience as the years go on. And now that we have *Countdown* in a book, there's no need to wait until 4.30 for a daily fix!

Good luck. I warn you, these puzzles require some application and dedication. They're fun but not for the fainthearted. And if you do well and think you could have a bash at the real thing, well, who knows, we might meet up in the *Countdown* studio.

All the best,
Richard Whiteley

Introduction

by the Executive Producer

When I took control of *Countdown* 15 months ago, I did so with pleasure, excitement and a great deal of pride. *Countdown* is a phenomenon, a phenomenon that was born out of, and has been established on, simplicity. To create and sustain such a piece of work takes dedicated professionals. Richard, Carol and the present production team are as professional as they come and are a joy to work with. I thank them for all their patience and efforts.

Producing Channel 4's top five shows of the week on a regular basis is something that you, the viewer, and we at Yorkshire Television should be very proud of. However, with success can come complacency – we must keep looking to the future. We owe it to the millions of viewers who watch every day to keep one step ahead The multimedia generation beckons, we must embrace it, we must not fear it. As Peter Lewis wrote in the *New York Times*, 'The real importance of multimedia is not in the hardware ... but in the software, just as the real significance of television is not in the picture tube but in the programming.' That is precisely the reason that we, in television, must get bolder, not more timid, in the years ahead. Enjoy

Jim Brown, Executive Producer

The rules of the game

In the programme, *Countdown* consists of 9 games – 6 letters games, 2 numbers games and a conundrum – in the following order:

1 Letters game – champion chooses letters
2 Letters game – challenger chooses letters
3 Letters game – champion chooses letters
4 Numbers game – challenger chooses numbers
5 Letters game – challenger chooses letters
6 Letters game – champion chooses letters
7 Letters game – challenger chooses letters
8 Numbers game – champion chooses numbers
9 Conundrum – on the buzzer

Letters games

- A contestant selects 9 letters from two piles of face-down cards (1 containing consonants, the other vowels).
- Each selection of 9 letters must contain at least 3 vowels and at least 4 consonants.
- When the last letter has been selected, the clock is started, and both contestants have 30 seconds to come up with the longest word they can make from the available letters.
- Each letter may be used only once.
- Only the longest word scores.
- Scoring: 1 point per letter, except for 9-letter words which score 18 points.

e.g. A L E R S T G I N

Contestant A offers STEALING for 8.
Contestant B wins with TRIANGLES for 9, which
doubles up to 18 points.

Score:
Contestant A: 0
Contestant B: 18

Numbers games

- One contestant selects 6 numbers from a selection of 24.
- There are 4 rows of numbers to select from; the top row
  contains the numbers 25, 50, 75 and 100; the other three
  rows contain the numbers 1–10 (two of each) at random.
- A random 3-digit target (from 100 to 999) is set and both
  contestants have 30 seconds to achieve this target, using
  only the four basic disciplines of addition, subtraction,
  division and multiplication. (No powers, fractions,
  decimals etc.)
- Contestants may use any or all of the numbers but may
  use each number only once.

e.g.   Numbers: 25 7 4 9 2 4   Target: 654

          Solution 1: $(7 \times 4) - 2 = 26$
                        $26 \times 25 = 650$
                        $650 + 4 = 654$

          Solution 2: $(4 \times 25) + 9 = 109$
                        $4 + 2 = 6$
                        $109 \times 6 = 654$

Scoring:
Spot on target: 10 points
Within 5:   7 points
Within 10:   5 points
More than 10 away: 0 points

Conundrums

- A board revolves to reveal a jumbled up 9-letter word. The contestants then have 30 seconds to decipher the word.
- This round is on the buzzer, and the first contestant to buzz and correctly state the 9-letter word is awarded 10 points.
- If the first person to buzz gives an incorrect answer, the other contestant then has the remaining time left on the clock to solve the Conundrum.

e.g. CHINALUNG = LAUNCHING
      TOMCRUISE = COSTUMIER

TIPS

Letters

- Look for common endings in the words: –ing, –ed, –iest, etc.
- If you have a choice between an unusual word and a common word of the same length, go for the common one – it's less likely to be rejected by Dictionary Corner!
- Never choose more than four vowels – ideally, choose five consonants and three vowels and then take a second or so before choosing your last letter to see if a word springs to mind.

Numbers

- Try to write your numbers solution down – it is surprising how many people forget just exactly how they reached a target!
- It is often beneficial to add or subtract one or more

small numbers from the larger number before multiplying or dividing.
- Check to see if the target number is exactly divisible by one of the six numbers that you have chosen.

How to use this book

The *Countdown* letters game

Try and make the longest word you can by using the letters in the selection given. Each letter may only be used once. You should allow yourself just 30 seconds for each round, but if you want to take longer then, hey, it's your book!

Proper nouns, hyphenated words and words with capitals are not allowed. You score 1 point for each letter that is used and 18 points if you make a 9-letter word.

e.g. A B C F I R T A E

Solution and scoring:

Fabricate – 9 letters (18 points)
Bacteria – 8 letters (8 points)
Cabaret – 7 letters (7 points)

The *Countdown* numbers game

You are given 6 numbers to work with that are your tools to help you reach the given target. Use any or all of the numbers but only use each number once. Only addition, multiplication, subtraction and division can be used to reach the target; and whole numbers only are allowed at all stages of your calculations.

Scoring:

Spot on target: 10 points
Within 5:   7 points
Within 10:   5 points

Solutions outside the range of 10 of the target do not score.

e.g. 100 4 6 7 9 3   Target: 515

$$100 - 9 - 4 = 87$$
$$87 \times 6 = 522$$
$$522 - 7 = 515 \ (10 \ points)$$

Countdown conundrum

Find the hidden 9-letter word from the letters given.

Correct solution scores 10 points.

e.g. E A S T E R E G G = SEGREGATE (10 points).

Hints and tips for playing the *Countdown* games

Letters games

There is no quick guide to success when it comes to finding long words. Firstly, you must know of the word – otherwise you'll never find it in the first place, so nobody is ever going to find the longest in every single round.

For example, in a selection of A A I I R H K T S, most people would struggle to get any further than shark. However, there is a 9-letter word, TARAHIKIS (fish), but unless you know of it, you are never going to find it.

However, you can increase your chances of success by looking for typical word endings that are commonplace in the English language.

Words ending in –iest, –er, –ing, –ted, etc, can often be found in selections; and trying to find words constructed like this is always a good place to start. Likewise, words starting with over–, out–, re– are often tucked away in there too.

Also, depending upon the letters in the selection, it can often be fruitful to pair together letters that have natural partners and see what can be made. For example, C + K, C + H, P + L etc.

Another tip is to always look out for double letters that can go together. Pairing together o's, e's, d's, l's, etc can yield some king-sized words. Remember that the letter 'S' is a valuable bonus that can help to make plurals, which means longer words.

Lastly, the best advice of all is that you enjoy tackling the puzzles and try to beat your own personal targets. So if your highest word ever is a 7, strive for the 8 and then aim to repeat it. Once you think you have what it takes, write to us for an application form and then wait and see what happens.

Conundrums

Most people are of the opinion that you either see them straight away or you don't get them at all. This is not really the best way to look at a conundrum. If you can't see it in 2 seconds flat, then spend the next 28 reworking the selection to see if something comes up.

Look for the endings, look for conundrums that are made up of two smaller words, e.g. CHEWLATER. You might find the word wheels then realise that the letters trac are left, making cars. Then, hey presto, you have CARTWHEEL.

Countdown competition

Win a fabulous trip to Yorkshire Television, where you and your guest will be treated to a VIP day out, which will include:

- Accommodation and travel.
- A *Countdown* goody bag.
- Meeting Richard and Carol.
- Seeing *Countdown* being recorded.
- A Commemorative photograph.

How to play

There are 9 questions that relate to *Countdown* in this book. Simply answer each question, then take the first letter from each answer and write it down.

If you correctly answer all 9 questions, you will be left with 9 letters. These 9 letters can be arranged to form the answer to our special competition conundrum.

The winner will be picked at random from all correct entries received before December 31, 2001.

Send your answer to Granada Media, 20 Mortimer Street, London, W1T 3JW, marked 'Countdown Competition'.

Round 1

LETTER GAME

1 | U | N | I | X | E | R | T | A | N |

| | | | | | | | | |

2 | G | I | E | D | V | I | S | C | S |

| | | | | | | | | |

3 | E | T | O | X | H | N | O | G | U |

| | | | | | | | | |

NUMBER GAME

| 25 | 2 | 3 | 5 | 7 | 9 | | 887 |

CONUNDRUM

| B | I | R | D | D | U | E | T | S |

Round 2

LETTER GAME

1 | L | R | K | C | A | E | E | M | F |

2 | F | A | D | I | O | G | E | R | N |

3 | B | R | I | S | H | E | N | D | A |

NUMBER GAME

| 25 | 6 | 2 | 3 | 4 | 4 | **852** |

CONUNDRUM

| P | I | N | K | G | R | O | O | V |

Round 3

LETTER GAME

1 O E W M N O F R G

2 N R E Y A B T O N

3 R D G E A E T B T

NUMBER GAME

50	25	6	3	3	2	667

CONUNDRUM

H A I L T H R E E

Round 4

LETTER GAME

1 | E | R | D | M | I | N | A | O | Z |

2 | R | I | N | G | C | O | W | E | L |

3 | J | A | E | D | I | E | T | N | C |

NUMBER GAME

| 50 | 75 | 9 | 1 | 3 | 4 | | **720** |

CONUNDRUM

| D | E | A | L | T | H | R | E | E |

Round 5

LETTER GAME

1 | T | L | A | R | K | E | E | N | M |

| | | | | | | | | |

2 | N | U | T | N | F | I | A | E | O |

| | | | | | | | | |

3 | B | E | I | H | S | T | O | I | V |

| | | | | | | | | |

NUMBER GAME

| 25 | 8 | 10 | 4 | 6 | 2 | | **824** |

CONUNDRUM

| T | A | R | D | Y | E | Y | E | S |

Round 6

LETTER GAME

1

K	I	H	A	D	E	V	S	E

2

O	B	L	A	D	I	M	Y	C

3

Q	U	S	E	I	D	L	F	I

NUMBER GAME

25	1	6	8	9	1	838

CONUNDRUM

L	A	N	K	G	R	I	P	S

Round 7

LETTER GAME

1

G	Y	O	O	B	R	I	E	N

2

S	C	U	O	R	A	B	I	L

3

G	N	J	O	I	S	N	A	C

NUMBER GAME

25	8	7	2	2	4		888

CONUNDRUM

A	N	S	W	E	R	S	E	A

Round 8

LETTER GAME

1 | H | U | B | E | A | S | R | D | N |

2 | N | L | E | U | C | A | R | E | L |

3 | D | C | I | N | D | O | R | E | R |

NUMBER GAME

| 100 | 10 | 8 | 7 | 8 | 10 | **246** |

CONUNDRUM

| E | A | R | T | H | C | L | A | D |

Game 1

Match yourself against ...

Scott Mearns (Series 41 champion)

Round 1	M V D E A T N O R
Round 2	H S I E A B N Y U
Round 3	S D T I E M P A R
Round 4	100 75 4 3 3 6 (570)
Round 5	E I W G D G A Z R
Round 6	M T O E A G S N I
Round 7	C N D E A X T E R
Round 8	50 75 100 25 10 2 (161)
Round 9	GINRAPPER

Round 9

LETTER GAME

1

I	S	T	A	F	E	M	N	O

2

H	O	C	U	S	A	I	G	N

3

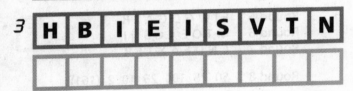

H	B	I	E	I	S	V	T	N

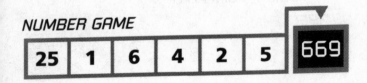

NUMBER GAME

25	1	6	4	2	5	**669**

CONUNDRUM

E	M	P	R	E	S	S	D	I

Round 10

LETTER GAME

1

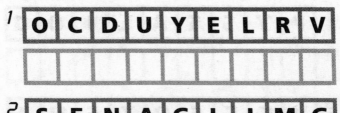

O	C	D	U	Y	E	L	R	V

2

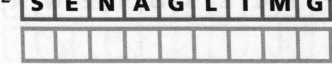

S	E	N	A	G	L	I	M	G

3

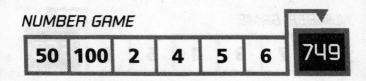

E	A	S	S	M	I	T	R	F

NUMBER GAME

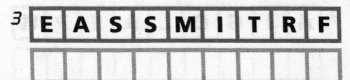

50	100	2	4	5	6	**749**

CONUNDRUM

R	O	S	E	C	R	O	P	S

Round 11

LETTER GAME

1

P	Y	S	T	A	L	I	O	C

2

V	C	E	S	O	T	E	N	A

3

A	I	G	D	L	A	E	P	W

NUMBER GAME

25	7	3	1	5	9	666

CONUNDRUM

P	A	S	T	L	I	C	K	S

12

Round 12

LETTER GAME

1 | N | H | N | I | A | R | M | E | K |

| | | | | | | | | |

2 | N | E | E | O | X | Y | T | A | G |

| | | | | | | | | |

3 | E | T | R | U | B | T | M | S | A |

| | | | | | | | | |

NUMBER GAME

| 100 | 50 | 10 | 8 | 4 | 7 | | 925 |

CONUNDRUM

| P | O | L | A | R | A | N | E | E |

Round 13

LETTER GAME

1 | T | G | I | A | N | R | U | Y | A |

| | | | | | | | | |

2 | H | L | V | R | A | O | E | M | T |

| | | | | | | | | |

3 | S | C | N | K | I | U | M | E | T |

| | | | | | | | | |

NUMBER GAME

| 75 | 25 | 100 | 4 | 2 | 9 | **692** |

CONUNDRUM

| G | I | A | N | T | P | U | G | S |

14

Round 14

LETTER GAME

1

V	R	F	G	O	I	L	D	E

2

L	S	G	O	U	D	I	R	E

3

M	T	O	A	S	B	E	R	N

NUMBER GAME

100	7	5	5	4	3	946

CONUNDRUM

S	L	A	M	C	H	E	S	T

Round 15

LETTER GAME

1 | U | D | L | F | R | O | W | E | P |

| | | | | | | | | | |

2 | F | P | N | A | Y | O | L | M | E |

| | | | | | | | | | |

3 | A | I | T | E | N | D | U | Q | A |

| | | | | | | | | | |

NUMBER GAME

| 75 | 50 | 25 | 7 | 2 | 8 | **530** |

CONUNDRUM

| P | R | I | M | E | G | E | N | T |

16

Round 16

LETTER GAME

1
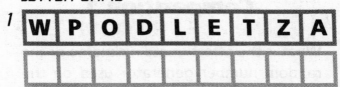

W	P	O	D	L	E	T	Z	A

2

R	S	R	M	E	O	A	P	T

3

G	R	E	A	L	W	A	Y	D

NUMBER GAME

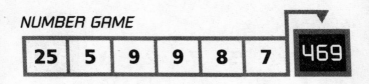

25	5	9	9	8	7	**469**

CONUNDRUM

T	I	M	E	D	A	T	E	D

Competition 1

What is the affectionate nickname of the random number generator used on the show?

Round 17

LETTER GAME

1

E	F	G	H	I	L	W	T	Y

2

O	K	R	Y	B	A	N	D	E

3

L	B	E	Y	S	A	T	R	E

NUMBER GAME

100	1	1	2	2	3	927

CONUNDRUM

P	R	E	S	S	D	I	E	D

Round 18

LETTER GAME

1 | N | S | M | E | U | C | O | E | P |

2 | N | R | L | U | E | O | Y | S | D |

3 | B | E | U | F | G | I | R | Q | T |

NUMBER GAME

| 75 | 100 | 8 | 4 | 2 | 6 | **719** |

CONUNDRUM

| A | C | E | F | I | B | R | E | S |

Round 19

LETTER GAME

1 | R | U | L | P | D | I | A | V | E |

2 | J | H | E | N | B | L | I | O | T |

3 | P | G | S | N | P | O | T | E | A |

NUMBER GAME

| 100 | 4 | 7 | 8 | 1 | 6 | **288** |

CONUNDRUM

| T | R | E | E | F | I | N | E | R |

Round 20

LETTER GAME

1

E	L	I	M	N	A	N	Y	V

2

H	M	O	E	O	I	S	N	F

3

S	I	P	O	T	C	H	L	I

NUMBER GAME

75	50	25	100	4	3	554

CONUNDRUM

U	N	D	E	R	J	O	E	Y

Round 21

LETTER GAME

1

L	S	B	T	N	U	I	E	E	D

2

C	T	X	W	E	I	E	O	R

3

S	U	B	A	D	O	R	I	N

NUMBER GAME

50	8	3	5	8	1	**756**

CONUNDRUM

G	E	R	M	A	N	H	I	P

Round 22

LETTER GAME

1 | G | B | R | S | I | E | F | U | G |
|---|---|---|---|---|---|---|---|---|
| | | | | | | | | |

2 | H | E | N | O | W | S | B | I | T |
|---|---|---|---|---|---|---|---|---|
| | | | | | | | | |

3 | T | U | D | O | G | E | R | A | S |
|---|---|---|---|---|---|---|---|---|
| | | | | | | | | |

NUMBER GAME

75	50	6	8	4	9	**483**

CONUNDRUM

W	H	I	T	E	R	O	S	E

Round 23

LETTER GAME

1 W R A C B E U L G

2 N S R C E I W E Y

3 L A M B O R D I E

NUMBER GAME

| 25 | 2 | 7 | 9 | 10 | 5 | **992** |

CONUNDRUM

R I N C O N J U G

Round 24

LETTER GAME

1

A	J	R	E	B	O	W	T	O

2

T	M	I	E	D	A	F	I	W

3

E	Y	O	R	L	I	P	A	T

NUMBER GAME

100	7	7	4	10	8	**596**

CONUNDRUM

F	R	E	A	K	B	A	T	S

Game 2

Match yourself against ...

Allan Saldanha (Series 15 finalist)

Round 1	L N K O I I G A S
Round 2	N B L A E T P I Y
Round 3	T K M O A E P T N
Round 4	100 10 3 9 9 2 (581)
Round 5	G R N A I T R E C
Round 6	B X T A U I T O N
Round 7	G F Y E I S N A S
Round 8	25 10 9 10 5 8 (562)
Round 9	IPULLONTO

Round 25

LETTER GAME

1

J	O	T	W	A	N	S	E	B

2

D	B	E	A	T	S	L	U	W

3

A	H	M	U	R	N	E	E	J

NUMBER GAME

50	5	4	3	1	3	801

CONUNDRUM

D	E	L	L	A	R	I	P	S

Round 26

LETTER GAME

1

O	D	R	Y	U	R	S	V	E

2

A	I	T	H	K	R	C	S	O

3

S	H	S	R	W	I	O	A	T

NUMBER GAME

50	25	75	6	5	7	**417**

CONUNDRUM

B	O	R	E	S	H	A	C	K

Round 27

LETTER GAME

1

A	S	C	T	O	R	V	R	E

2

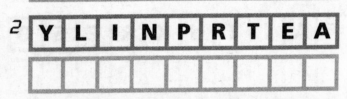

Y	L	I	N	P	R	T	E	A

3

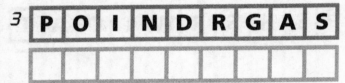

P	O	I	N	D	R	G	A	S

NUMBER GAME

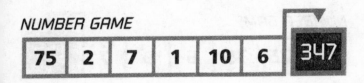

75	2	7	1	10	6	**347**

CONUNDRUM

P	R	A	W	N	S	P	E	E

Round 28

LETTER GAME

1
A	M	I	U	M	E	D	S	L

2
G	A	I	R	M	Y	E	S	T

3
M	L	C	E	I	N	O	X	A

NUMBER GAME

5	6	3	3	4	4	271

CONUNDRUM

S	T	U	M	P	F	I	R	E

Round 29

LETTER GAME

1

R	S	O	M	A	E	T	B	D

2

K	L	D	Y	T	E	A	E	C

3

C	E	I	D	P	R	Q	U	E

NUMBER GAME

25	5	10	10	1	5		864

CONUNDRUM

D	E	A	D	L	Y	H	O	I

Round 30

LETTER GAME

1

F	Y	S	Z	E	U	I	P	T

2

C	S	N	A	E	O	P	L	A

3

R	I	P	T	C	U	S	E	R

NUMBER GAME

25	3	7	2	4	5	980

CONUNDRUM

L	I	V	I	D	I	C	E	S

Round 31

LETTER GAME

1

T	A	R	E	P	O	C	H	N

2

T	S	L	E	A	I	B	O	P

3

S	D	U	E	T	Z	Y	O	W

NUMBER GAME

100	3	8	4	7	2	574

CONUNDRUM

E	V	A	T	U	R	N	E	D

Round 32

LETTER GAME

1

E	D	R	I	T	G	F	U	

2

N	E	V	I	O	L	B	O	I

3

T	G	H	O	E	S	A	S	H

NUMBER GAME

75	6	5	8	4	9	**951**

CONUNDRUM

B	L	A	M	E	G	O	L	D

Competition 2

What is the Christian name of a *Countdown* favourite, much loved for his magical contributions and brainteasers.

Round 33

LETTER GAME

1

P	A	O	R	T	X	H	S	E

2

E	S	Y	T	A	L	C	N	R

3

V	R	I	E	I	L	M	N	F

NUMBER GAME

75	25	50	6	7	9	**665**

CONUNDRUM

G	E	C	K	O	P	I	N	T

Round 34

LETTER GAME

1 | M | G | W | L | I | O | D | E | A |

2 | T | E | S | O | D | G | T | A | S |

3 | E | D | I | M | L | C | T | E | A |

NUMBER GAME

| 10 | 9 | 4 | 5 | 2 | 7 | **760** |

CONUNDRUM

| T | R | A | D | L | A | D | Y | S |

Round 35

LETTER GAME

1 | D | A | I | L | E | I | F | N | Z |

| | | | | | | | | |

2 | G | R | Y | O | R | U | A | P | T |

| | | | | | | | | |

3 | S | P | B | A | U | O | M | G | S |

| | | | | | | | | |

NUMBER GAME

| 7 | 7 | 5 | 5 | 3 | 3 | **444** |

CONUNDRUM

| T | I | A | H | E | L | I | U | M |

Round 36

LETTER GAME

1

A	Y	E	F	D	P	R	M	I

2

A	B	D	I	L	O	V	T	E

3

D	E	U	R	T	O	G	R	S

NUMBER GAME

25	8	8	6	4	5	383

CONUNDRUM

I	N	T	O	D	I	N	E	R

Round 37

LETTER GAME

1

R	T	O	P	C	B	L	A	I

2

T	Y	P	O	S	T	R	E	A

3

L	K	Y	O	O	A	S	C	P

NUMBER GAME

100	5	10	4	6	1	747

CONUNDRUM

M	O	N	O	M	U	N	I	C

Round 38

LETTER GAME

1 G E T O D A R D E

2 F B U I O L T R A

3 H L G A E I T L N

NUMBER GAME

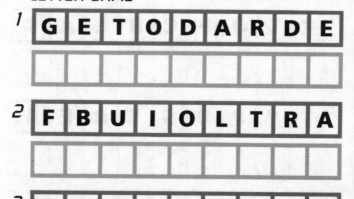

| 50 | 9 | 7 | 4 | 9 | 7 | 602 |

CONUNDRUM

E V I L G R I P E

Round 39

LETTER GAME

1

D	Y	L	H	I	T	S	O	A

2

O	F	S	G	I	X	D	E	H

3

B	G	A	O	S	Z	P	E	A

NUMBER GAME

25	6	3	9	2	4	**938**

CONUNDRUM

R	I	P	E	G	R	A	I	N

Round 40

LETTER GAME

1

S	U	E	Q	Y	B	R	A	L

2

E	D	H	L	E	A	T	F	I

3

T	R	I	D	A	N	K	W	E

NUMBER GAME

25	7	1	6	9	2	**478**

CONUNDRUM

C	L	E	A	N	C	O	D	E

Game 3

Match yourself against ...

Liz Barber (Series 20 champion)

Round 1   S T Q D A O E H B
Round 2   F L S R I A U C I
Round 3   Y D T L E I E D P

Round 4   50 8 7 5 1 10 (134)

Round 5   S C Z S O U I A P
Round 6   P M L D I E E R J
Round 7   T Y R D I A O B T

Round 8   25 8 1 5 8 4 (162)

Round 9   DRIEDPOTS

Round 41

LETTER GAME

1 | L | L | W | O | E | S | I | R | T |
|---|---|---|---|---|---|---|---|---|
| | | | | | | | | |

2 | F | T | W | E | O | E | S | L | N |
|---|---|---|---|---|---|---|---|---|
| | | | | | | | | |

3 | L | P | U | E | E | T | I | D | N |
|---|---|---|---|---|---|---|---|---|
| | | | | | | | | |

NUMBER GAME

25	8	4	3	3	6	**527**

CONUNDRUM

D	E	T	T	I	B	E	L	L

Round 42

LETTER GAME

1

A	D	A	C	W	K	R	B	E

2

D	C	R	A	S	P	I	E	P

3

N	O	G	N	I	S	E	A	D

NUMBER GAME

75	1	2	3	4	5	704

CONUNDRUM

C	A	N	D	I	D	O	T	I

Round 43

LETTER GAME

1

A	P	D	L	U	A	R	G	E

2

R	S	B	I	O	T	D	E	O

3

V	T	E	A	M	U	L	A	F

NUMBER GAME

100	8	2	3	7	4	**966**

CONUNDRUM

E	V	I	L	B	E	I	N	G

Round 44

LETTER GAME

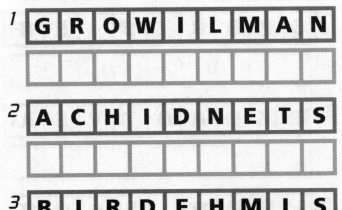

1 G R O W I L M A N

2 A C H I D N E T S

3 B I R D E H M I S

NUMBER GAME

| 10 | 6 | 7 | 5 | 5 | 3 | 963 |

CONUNDRUM

T E A T U L I P S

Round 45

LETTER GAME

1 | C | P | B | R | Y | E | I | E | R |

2 | R | M | D | A | O | T | V | E | A |

3 | S | N | O | D | I | F | A | G | H |

NUMBER GAME

| 25 | 4 | 1 | 9 | 6 | 2 | **333** |

CONUNDRUM

| L | U | N | A | R | V | I | S | E |

Round 46

LETTER GAME

1

C	O	B	R	E	L	O	E	H

2

F	A	D	E	G	T	O	P	O

3

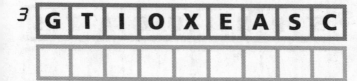

G	T	I	O	X	E	A	S	C

NUMBER GAME

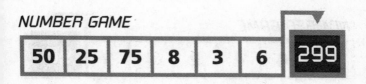

50	25	75	8	3	6	299

CONUNDRUM

C	U	T	E	F	A	U	L	T

Round 47

LETTER GAME

1

D	O	S	R	I	W	O	N	D

2

F	A	L	R	Y	U	P	E	I

3

T	P	N	I	U	O	A	T	S

NUMBER GAME

100	4	4	2	1	3	960

CONUNDRUM

G	I	N	S	T	U	P	I	D

Round 48

LETTER GAME

1

S	U	O	L	V	I	C	E	S

2
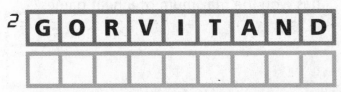

G	O	R	V	I	T	A	N	D

3
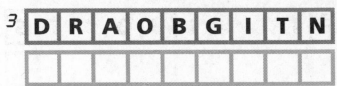

D	R	A	O	B	G	I	T	N

NUMBER GAME

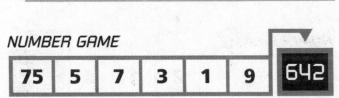

75	5	7	3	1	9	**642**

CONUNDRUM

M	A	N	I	C	A	B	L	E

Competition 3

What is the word, coined by Richard Whiteley, that refers to a contestant who has won the maximum of 8 heat games?

Round 49

LETTER GAME

1

O	S	C	H	A	Z	E	P	Y

2

G	M	R	A	E	N	C	O	H

3

T	I	A	R	J	C	O	S	A

NUMBER GAME

8	5	2	1	9	9	**748**

CONUNDRUM

C	L	A	W	T	H	R	E	E

Round 50

LETTER GAME

1

B	T	A	A	C	L	E	H	E

2

E	L	T	D	T	E	E	R	A

3

O	E	I	N	B	V	H	A	G

NUMBER GAME

50	7	8	9	10	10	356

CONUNDRUM

G	I	V	E	R	O	U	N	D

Round 51

LETTER GAME

1

Y	B	G	F	A	A	U	E	R

2

S	M	T	E	S	P	U	D	I

3

O	M	L	A	R	T	I	U	S

NUMBER GAME

75	6	2	2	1	1	290

CONUNDRUM

C	I	L	L	A	S	B	I	T

Round 52

LETTER GAME

1 N I E R T H W A G

2 A D F E I N R D R

3 N R E Y A B T O N

NUMBER GAME

| 25 | 2 | 6 | 6 | 3 | 2 | 785 |

CONUNDRUM

T O R N O F F E R

Round 53

LETTER GAME

1

N	G	T	E	A	O	B	I	J

2

R	D	G	E	A	E	T	V	T

3

K	T	U	E	S	L	E	G	Y

NUMBER GAME

50	5	1	3	4	1	686

CONUNDRUM

S	P	A	R	E	S	U	D	S

Round 54

LETTER GAME

1 J N S U A C E N T

2 G R I E A N W N E

3 B T Y R I I S C A

NUMBER GAME

| 100 | 2 | 9 | 7 | 10 | 10 | **404** |

CONUNDRUM

D U D R E P O R T

Round 55

LETTER GAME

1 `E H E I L D A N W`

2 `R O N E T J U I P`

3 `O B S L A E M R C`

NUMBER GAME

`7` `2` `8` `5` `6` `2` **904**

CONUNDRUM

`D O E L I L A C S`

Round 56

LETTER GAME

1

P	L	G	O	D	I	A	U	E

2

A	N	Y	I	V	T	E	L	O

3

S	O	A	V	G	E	I	S	E

NUMBER GAME

75	10	4	8	1	5	779

CONUNDRUM

K	N	E	W	A	G	E	N	I

Game 4

Match yourself against ...

Harvey Freeman (All-time Supreme Champion)

Round 1	N T R U A E Z I S
Round 2	E D A C G E L I N
Round 3	D K C E O A V N E
Round 4	25 5 10 2 7 1 (728)
Round 5	Y O R I M O T J E
Round 6	F L R I A O W A S
Round 7	D M E H O N G I E
Round 8	100 7 5 4 10 1 (783)
Round 9	NICESLONE

Round 57

LETTER GAME

1 | T | S | O | E | A | C | J | N | I |

2 | K | A | T | J | E | A | T | D | N |

3 | E | B | H | A | M | O | N | D | R |

NUMBER GAME

| 25 | 2 | 3 | 1 | 10 | 9 | **462** |

CONUNDRUM

| L | O | G | O | R | A | M | U | S |

Round 58

LETTER GAME

1
B	I	M	O	N	A	L	M	A

2
L	E	G	A	S	N	Y	I	C

3
N	A	P	E	J	R	O	Y	L

NUMBER GAME

100	10	1	8	3	8	716

CONUNDRUM

P	R	E	P	A	G	A	I	N

Round 59

LETTER GAME

1

L I M A H I G S R

2

K S U P G A O D E

3

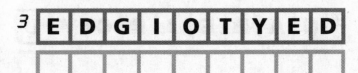

E D G I O T Y E D

NUMBER GAME

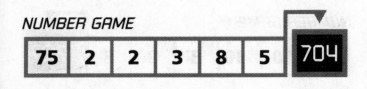

75 2 2 3 8 5 — 704

CONUNDRUM

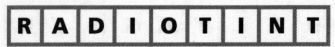

R A D I O T I N T

Round 60

LETTER GAME

1

U	P	N	T	I	A	K	D	O

2

Z	I	U	E	N	X	A	S	D

3

Q	S	B	O	I	A	T	R	U

NUMBER GAME

50	4	10	5	10	3	987

CONUNDRUM

T	E	L	Y	A	N	G	E	L

Round 61

LETTER GAME

1

F	G	R	O	I	E	S	H	L

2

Y	V	U	S	D	I	E	N	T

3

W	N	T	U	O	N	A	R	E

NUMBER GAME

25	50	100	6	6	9	**693**

CONUNDRUM

F	E	T	I	D	S	U	P	E

Round 62

LETTER GAME

1

| A | V | T | I | R | E | D | L | U |

2

| S | N | E | A | G | L | M | I | G |

3

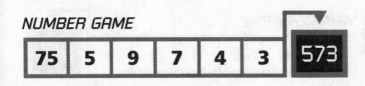

| N | G | T | R | C | A | O | B | I |

NUMBER GAME

| 75 | 5 | 9 | 7 | 4 | 3 | **573** |

CONUNDRUM

| D | I | R | T | Y | R | O | O | M |

Round 63

LETTER GAME

1
E	A	S	S	M	I	T	R	F

2
I	E	R	F	B	T	O	S	E

3
B	G	E	I	R	D	S	U	P

NUMBER GAME

50	6	8	8	1	7	867

CONUNDRUM

A	N	T	T	I	L	O	P	E

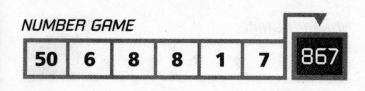

70

Round 64

LETTER GAME

1

N	D	E	A	M	L	I	W	R

2

N	O	I	N	I	T	F	G	Y

3

E	I	M	N	Q	S	T	U	Y

NUMBER GAME

25	50	7	9	2	3	**944**

CONUNDRUM

F	O	R	D	C	O	M	E	T

Competition 4

On the show's closing credits, you will see 'by arrangement with _____ Stellman'. What is the missing word?

Round 65

LETTER GAME

1 | Y | A | C | D | G | T | E | R | O |

| | | | | | | | | |

2 | A | C | E | E | I | F | N | R | T |

| | | | | | | | | |

3 | U | L | T | R | A | L | I | B | Y |

| | | | | | | | | |

NUMBER GAME

| 100 | 75 | 50 | 4 | 10 | 5 | **885** |

CONUNDRUM

| I | T | I | S | Q | U | E | E | R |

Round 66

LETTER GAME

1

G	I	F	A	T	O	U	E	R

2

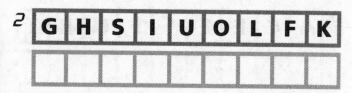

G	H	S	I	U	O	L	F	K

3

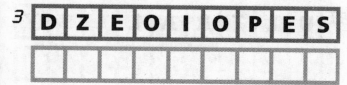

D	Z	E	O	I	O	P	E	S

NUMBER GAME

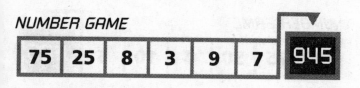

75	25	8	3	9	7	**945**

CONUNDRUM

T	R	I	A	D	R	I	T	E

Round 67

LETTER GAME

1

C	S	I	N	A	R	P	E	N

2

M	A	R	T	Y	O	R	N	E

3

H	I	S	V	E	R	O	T	L

NUMBER GAME

50	6	8	2	1	3	867

CONUNDRUM

G	L	E	N	D	R	O	O	P

Round 68

LETTER GAME

1

T	L	R	I	E	G	M	A	R

2

H	I	N	S	A	G	L	O	T

3

B	E	R	Y	T	U	N	A	C

NUMBER GAME

25	7	5	4	1	10	628

CONUNDRUM

T	Y	P	I	C	A	L	E	S

Round 69

LETTER GAME

1

S	A	R	T	O	E	S	K	B

2

N	B	N	E	A	I	L	P	S

3

E	A	I	B	Y	T	R	N	H

NUMBER GAME

10	9	10	8	7	7	**226**

CONUNDRUM

W	R	O	N	G	H	A	I	R

Round 70

LETTER GAME

1

G	J	L	E	A	I	S	D	F

2

P	R	A	D	O	T	A	T	E

3

U	R	V	I	L	E	T	O	R

NUMBER GAME

100	1	9	1	7	4	555

CONUNDRUM

L	O	N	G	T	U	L	I	P

Round 71

LETTER GAME

1

T	I	M	L	O	P	E	D	S

2

L	K	T	A	E	P	R	A	C

3

S	P	O	I	H	N	E	C	A

NUMBER GAME

8	3	4	1	2	3	864

CONUNDRUM

H	O	L	Y	B	O	S	C	O

Round 72

LETTER GAME

1 N G H E I E D T N

2 T S V N O I U D A

3 O A T F B N K U G

NUMBER GAME

| 4 | 5 | 2 | 3 | 1 | 6 | 840 |

CONUNDRUM

T I N Y T A M E R

Game 5

Match yourself against ...

Kate Ogilvie (Series 39 champion)

Round 1   F V N A E C P I R
Round 2   F O U G S M E L T
Round 3   T S N A O E D R M

Round 4   75 8 2 6 10 5 (454)

Round 5   A I K S O D E H R
Round 6   D B N A I E M G N
Round 7   T R A U O Y G Q C

Round 8   25 4 9 5 10 8 (643)

Round 9   RIGWINTER

Round 73

LETTER GAME

1

G	Z	N	U	E	A	S	L	D

2

A	L	B	O	T	E	R	E	I

3

F	O	G	A	H	O	Y	R	L

NUMBER GAME

100	6	7	2	2	5	**372**

CONUNDRUM

L	I	L	A	C	S	A	C	S

Round 74

LETTER GAME

1 | E | N | V | U | I | J | S | K | R |

2 | E | O | E | B | N | T | Y | A | G |

3 | S | R | E | O | M | M | E | T | I |

NUMBER GAME

| 50 | 6 | 10 | 2 | 9 | 7 | **871** |

CONUNDRUM

| D | A | D | S | B | O | N | C | E |

Round 75

LETTER GAME

1 N L R E U S G W A

2 B O P D A N G I R

3 G R A F I C B E N

NUMBER GAME

| 75 | 25 | 50 | 100 | 4 | 9 | **606** |

CONUNDRUM

F L E E T D A R T

Round 76

LETTER GAME

1 | O | S | T | E | Y | R | A | B | U |

2 | S | B | I | A | S | T | O | U | S |

3 | A | E | L | I | G | S | A | C | L |

NUMBER GAME

| 25 | 10 | 7 | 4 | 4 | 2 | | 812 |

CONUNDRUM

| T | H | I | S | G | N | O | M | E |

Round 77

LETTER GAME

1 C R E I D O L V Y

2 C M S A E O G U L

3 W E R I H C E B X

NUMBER GAME

| 50 | 100 | 8 | 7 | 9 | 10 | 311 |

CONUNDRUM

H E A R P O E M S

Round 78

LETTER GAME

1 | L | R | N | O | U | E | Y | S | F |

| | | | | | | | | |

2 | R | N | A | T | G | O | D | C | E |

| | | | | | | | | |

3 | L | S | G | I | A | E | P | T | N |

| | | | | | | | | |

NUMBER GAME

| 25 | 2 | 9 | 1 | 1 | 6 | | 347 |

CONUNDRUM

| A | N | G | L | O | H | U | M | P |

Round 79

LETTER GAME

1

B	S	U	X	R	E	L	E	H	A

2

A	A	C	D	E	I	L	L	N

3

C	E	I	L	N	O	Q	U	X

NUMBER GAME

50	7	10	8	8	5	**933**

CONUNDRUM

B	E	N	D	I	F	E	E	T

Round 80

LETTER GAME

1

B	E	I	O	R	S	T	U	V

2

O	C	A	T	G	E	H	P	D

3

V	E	R	H	E	N	F	I	G

NUMBER GAME

25	4	1	10	10	1	**875**

CONUNDRUM

G	O	L	D	E	N	A	C	E

Competition 5

The highest score ever achieved on a 9-round show is?

LETTER GAME

1
A	S	K	R	O	L	Y	C	I

2
L	R	Z	L	U	E	I	G	Y

3
R	N	Q	O	A	U	C	S	I

NUMBER GAME

50	75	2	3	1	9	186

CONUNDRUM

M	I	S	T	Y	T	O	N	E

Round 82

LETTER GAME

1

L	G	A	I	P	S	A	R	B

2

L	R	Z	O	A	E	R	M	T

3

A	I	O	N	R	Y	T	C	V

NUMBER GAME

75	8	10	9	8	9	**244**

CONUNDRUM

E	D	D	Y	H	A	R	T	E

Round 83

LETTER GAME

1 | O | E | I | T | F | S | X | A | D |

| | | | | | | | | |

2 | G | D | C | I | A | E | O | T | B |

| | | | | | | | | |

3 | T | H | M | U | L | U | O | R | F |

| | | | | | | | | |

NUMBER GAME

| 10 | 3 | 2 | 8 | 9 | 1 | **584** |

CONUNDRUM

| S | A | T | I | N | C | A | F | E |

Round 84

LETTER GAME

1 | A | Y | D | E | I | O | V | P | L |

2 | Y | H | M | T | P | U | I | D | E |

3 | E | R | P | I | M | T | C | E | F |

NUMBER GAME

| 25 | 10 | 2 | 4 | 7 | 2 | **555** |

CONUNDRUM

| I | M | N | O | G | H | O | S | T |

LETTER GAME

1

S	F	R	L	H	O	U	I	E

2

T	R	T	I	E	I	D	V	D

3

S	G	A	C	O	S	I	T	D

NUMBER GAME

6	7	4	4	3	1	**294**

CONUNDRUM

D	A	W	N	K	H	O	R	I

Round 86

LETTER GAME

1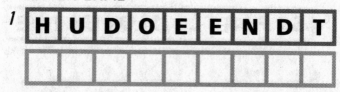

H U D O E E N D T

2

F L A C D I E Y L

3

O E S F T I D S U

NUMBER GAME

| 100 | 50 | 5 | 10 | 3 | 7 | 639 |

CONUNDRUM

S C A N T N O N O

Round 87

LETTER GAME

1 | G | R | T | A | D | I | S | E | S |

2 | C | E | L | E | D | A | T | A | S |

3 | R | U | T | Y | O | I | P | A | L |

NUMBER GAME

| 75 | 25 | 100 | 50 | 2 | 2 | **704** |

CONUNDRUM

| D | A | D | O | T | U | N | E | S |

Round 88

LETTER GAME

1 | O | G | H | A | I | T | L | R | S |

2 | D | R | A | I | W | I | G | N | P |

3 | B | M | O | A | G | N | E | R | O |

NUMBER GAME

| 100 | 10 | 5 | 6 | 9 | 2 | **471** |

CONUNDRUM

| S | A | U | C | E | T | O | F | F |

Game 6

Match yourself against ...

David Elias (Series 27 champion)

Round 1   B S T O E A V D T
Round 2   S N T A E I X C O
Round 3   L G M E E A F R Y

Round 4   75 4 3 3 25 50 (520)

Round 5   H C B I E S T A S
Round 6   K L R E I O N L M
Round 7   D H R A V U O U M

Round 8   25 3 7 1 1 2 (509)

Round 9   HARKSINKS

Round 89

LETTER GAME

1

N	O	S	I	H	O	A	R	U

2

D	C	U	E	W	S	O	I	D

3

R	S	C	A	O	A	T	P	I

NUMBER GAME

50	8	1	7	6	1	**239**

CONUNDRUM

T	E	N	N	T	O	N	I	C

Round 90

LETTER GAME

1 | L | E | P | S | E | Z | R | I | Y |

2 | P | E | L | I | M | T | U | R | C |

3 | O | S | I | R | C | O | E | V | R |

NUMBER GAME

| 75 | 100 | 2 | 4 | 9 | 7 | **578** |

CONUNDRUM

| D | E | P | T | S | T | O | R | E |

Round 91

LETTER GAME

1 A L U T O A V E N

2 N A R O F Y L E P

3 E L U I V O N S A

NUMBER GAME

50	25	75	3	6	8	623

CONUNDRUM

O U T L A P P E D

Round 92

LETTER GAME

1

L	W	O	D	S	L	I	O	E

2

E	I	G	Y	U	D	R	H	S

3

C	N	O	C	A	T	O	U	P

NUMBER GAME

25	2	8	7	7	5	914

CONUNDRUM

T	O	U	G	H	P	A	R	A

Round 93

LETTER GAME

1 | A | D | D | E | G | I | N | O | S |

2 | D | D | U | U | N | R | S | E | E |

3 | R | T | A | G | E | S | H | O | S |

NUMBER GAME

| 100 | 6 | 9 | 9 | 2 | 2 | | 826 |

CONUNDRUM

| V | E | N | I | C | E | R | A | G |

Round 94

LETTER GAME

1 Y D G I E I R N O

2 U E A R D W V L O

3 E H I O R S T W Z

NUMBER GAME

| 25 | 3 | 10 | 4 | 5 | 7 | 937 |

CONUNDRUM

D U N D E E P O X

Round 95

LETTER GAME

1 | E | I | J | N | O | S | S | T | T |

| | | | | | | | | |

2 | A | C | E | I | I | M | R | S | T |

| | | | | | | | | |

3 | L | E | R | H | O | E | W | Y | N |

| | | | | | | | | |

NUMBER GAME

| 5 | 2 | 7 | 9 | 7 | 9 | **144** |

CONUNDRUM

| T | I | N | Y | T | I | G | E | R |

Round 96

LETTER GAME

1

V	A	T	P	E	C	A	L	O

2

D	S	E	O	G	X	N	E	P

3

E	V	A	D	B	L	I	T	R

NUMBER GAME

25	50	75	100	3	3	**741**

CONUNDRUM

F	I	G	F	R	I	E	N	D

Competition 6

What is the name of the device used in Dictionary Corner to highlight unusual words?

Round 97

LETTER GAME

1
T	D	N	I	U	I	M	L	O

2
S	P	V	E	U	A	T	Z	S

3
G	R	I	M	O	P	A	D	A

NUMBER GAME

75	8	3	6	6	7	**948**

CONUNDRUM

T	H	E	I	R	D	U	M	P

Round 98

LETTER GAME

1 T A G L A V E O C

2 P I N D U S O R E

3 R U R C O S A T S

NUMBER GAME

50	4	4	2	3	6	**377**

CONUNDRUM

C O C O A R I N D

Round 99

LETTER GAME

1

G	U	R	E	S	I	L	O	G

2

X	U	J	O	I	B	K	E	D

3

R	F	R	C	I	U	O	L	O

NUMBER GAME

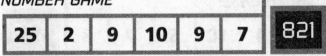

25	2	9	10	9	7	**821**

CONUNDRUM

C	A	N	C	E	L	H	I	T

Round 100

LETTER GAME

1

T	N	D	E	A	E	L	C	O

2

E	I	A	N	R	K	Z	S	N

3

A	T	I	D	P	N	Y	E	G

NUMBER GAME

25	4	10	5	7	3	**523**

CONUNDRUM

S	E	C	U	R	E	P	O	T

Round 101

LETTER GAME

1

S	M	R	N	I	E	U	A	R

2

L	T	O	A	N	D	C	B	E

3

E	T	X	C	O	I	L	V	S

NUMBER GAME

50	8	7	4	9	1	274

CONUNDRUM

D	O	G	N	I	F	F	E	N

Round 102

LETTER GAME

1 | O | E | I | D | N | R | A | R | N |

| | | | | | | | | |

2 | R | C | C | E | U | E | T | M | L |

| | | | | | | | | |

3 | D | S | C | A | R | N | I | T | E |

| | | | | | | | | |

NUMBER GAME

| 100 | 2 | 5 | 5 | 6 | 7 | **868** |

CONUNDRUM

| G | U | E | S | T | P | I | N | T |

Round 103

LETTER GAME

1

O	S	L	D	E	N	W	L	A

2

G	O	Y	R	E	H	U	D	N

3

T	H	O	R	S	Y	E	W	A

NUMBER GAME

75	6	3	8	8	3	697

CONUNDRUM

H	A	N	G	A	R	O	P	E

Round 104

LETTER GAME

1

H	U	G	L	A	N	S	E	I

2

A	V	E	N	D	U	G	R	E

3

S	V	A	O	H	R	A	X	E

NUMBER GAME

25	75	100	6	9	6	386

CONUNDRUM

C	R	U	E	L	B	A	I	T

Game 7

Match yourself against ...

Wayne Kelly (Series 28 finalist)

Round 1	L E G T A R U Q E
Round 2	O I S D L E T G A
Round 3	H O E P S K I A R
Round 4	7 1 3 9 2 25 (533)
Round 5	I E L T D O F S B
Round 6	N U C S A R M E S
Round 7	I A N P S R E N Y
Round 8	6 9 1 5 100 75 (920)
Round 9	ERICSRUFF

Round 105

LETTER GAME

1

E	O	T	R	I	A	N	D	P

2

O	F	S	R	E	C	G	U	T

3

O	S	I	N	I	S	N	A	T

NUMBER GAME

8	10	4	3	1	7	**875**

CONUNDRUM

N	O	V	A	G	R	I	P	P

Round 106

LETTER GAME

1
T	D	J	E	I	U	R	T	E

2
M	S	P	F	I	A	E	L	H

3
B	A	T	C	L	E	A	S	M

NUMBER GAME

100	75	6	2	5	1	464

CONUNDRUM

I	L	O	V	E	U	N	O	T

Round 107

LETTER GAME

1

P	R	N	I	E	R	S	I	F

2

G	E	T	N	G	O	R	A	B

3

N	D	R	A	I	U	S	P	E

NUMBER GAME

4	7	8	9	5	2	**253**

CONUNDRUM

M	I	N	C	E	M	A	S	H

Round 108

LETTER GAME

1

R	L	D	O	E	A	V	M	N

2

G	D	B	S	E	T	O	C	E

3

H	L	D	U	E	A	G	T	R

NUMBER GAME

50	3	2	10	4	8	642

CONUNDRUM

T	R	I	C	O	R	N	E	C

Round 109

LETTER GAME

1 | R | P | W | O | E | T | S | O | E |

2 | L | Y | P | R | U | E | E | I | Q |

3 | S | V | T | D | X | O | I | E | B |

NUMBER GAME

| 75 | 8 | 8 | 6 | 7 | 7 | **931** |

CONUNDRUM

| S | C | R | E | E | D | M | A | P |

Round 110

LETTER GAME

1 | T | Z | E | N | I | G | N | A | E |

| | | | | | | | | |

2 | Y | D | F | A | I | L | R | A | T |

| | | | | | | | | |

3 | C | I | N | C | O | A | T | R | S |

| | | | | | | | | |

NUMBER GAME

| 25 | 100 | 7 | 4 | 2 | 3 | | 620 |

CONUNDRUM

| A | S | K | F | O | R | G | I | N |

Round 111

LETTER GAME

1

M	T	S	H	O	O	R	A	D

2

G	I	C	A	E	T	K	O	D

3

N	I	E	P	S	Z	A	L	R

NUMBER GAME

25	1	6	7	8	8	**533**

CONUNDRUM

C	L	I	N	G	R	E	I	N

Round 112

LETTER GAME

1

P	F	A	E	R	D	I	M	E

2

S	C	S	T	O	E	I	R	X

3

L	G	F	O	A	L	E	R	T

NUMBER GAME

75	9	10	9	10	5	**444**

CONUNDRUM

S	P	E	E	D	B	A	R	D

Competition 7

How many contestants have appeared on the show and failed to score a single point?

Round 113

LETTER GAME

1 | B | N | A | C | O | T | G | E | S |

| | | | | | | | | |

2 | A | V | E | N | R | I | U | G | A |

| | | | | | | | | |

3 | T | S | P | D | E | A | I | E | T |

| | | | | | | | | |

NUMBER GAME

| 100 | 50 | 25 | 3 | 8 | 7 | 819 |

CONUNDRUM

| D | A | N | C | E | P | A | L | S |

Round 114

LETTER GAME

1 | M | L | T | I | E | O | J | R | S |

2 | F | T | S | T | I | E | U | A | M |

3 | S | F | I | O | A | M | N | V | U |

NUMBER GAME

| 50 | 9 | 6 | 4 | 10 | 6 | **914** |

CONUNDRUM

| O | G | R | E | Q | U | E | S | T |

Round 115

LETTER GAME

1 | R | H | Y | S | E | A | O | C | B |

| | | | | | | | | |

2 | G | R | P | Y | O | U | E | N | G |

| | | | | | | | | |

3 | T | S | R | A | E | T | M | O | Y |

| | | | | | | | | |

NUMBER GAME

| 25 | 5 | 2 | 3 | 2 | 8 | **777** |

CONUNDRUM

| L | O | V | E | N | U | R | S | Y |

Round 116

LETTER GAME

1 T R F O E I L Y R

2 O H E X I D A P E

3 E O U Z Y J T L T

NUMBER GAME

| 6 | 2 | 9 | 5 | 2 | 1 | **580** |

CONUNDRUM

S A T A N L I T E

Round 117

LETTER GAME

1 | S | R | T | M | F | O | A | O | K |

| | | | | | | | | |

2 | U | A | E | N | C | L | P | O | S |

| | | | | | | | | |

3 | N | L | E | G | G | E | F | E | I |

| | | | | | | | | |

NUMBER GAME

| 75 | 50 | 100 | 8 | 3 | 1 | **264** |

CONUNDRUM

| T | E | N | D | E | R | T | A | P |

Round 118

LETTER GAME

1 | T | A | U | R | H | L | R | B | E |

2 | D | E | S | R | U | M | O | W | G |

3 | I | E | A | H | S | T | N | B | P |

NUMBER GAME

| 25 | 2 | 6 | 3 | 5 | 1 | 882 |

CONUNDRUM

| R | O | L | L | O | W | H | I | P |

Round 119

LETTER GAME

1

T	O	R	I	E	I	F	V	L

2

R	M	D	E	I	T	S	A	U

3

B	S	J	Y	E	I	E	C	R

NUMBER GAME

9	7	4	2	1	6	**750**

CONUNDRUM

O	C	H	A	I	R	M	A	N

Round 120

LETTER GAME

1

U	C	E	D	P	I	G	N	N

2

A	S	C	O	O	G	R	E	L

3

S	N	G	O	I	I	R	S	O

NUMBER GAME

50	6	3	7	7	4	244

CONUNDRUM

D	A	R	N	S	C	E	N	T

Game 8

Match yourself against ...

Ray McPhie (Series 37 winner)

Round 1   T F D N Y I A E P
Round 2   L M U A N G E R I
Round 3   G D S N T E A E S

Round 4   100 2 10 6 7 4 (449)

Round 5   M R O E S D B A E
Round 6   V S C D Y A E O N
Round 7   G M W O U R P I E

Round 8   25 1 7 2 9 4 (731)

Round 9   LOUNGEMOO

Round 121

LETTER GAME

1 | L | M | W | O | E | O | E | N | T |

2 | L | R | E | E | A | G | S | C | L |

3 | Y | Q | L | U | I | T | A | M | U |

NUMBER GAME

| 25 | 2 | 4 | 3 | 3 | 5 | | 837 |

CONUNDRUM

| T | I | T | A | N | R | O | M | P |

Round 122

LETTER GAME

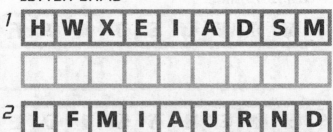

1 | H | W | X | E | I | A | D | S | M |

2 | L | F | M | I | A | U | R | N | D |

3 | S | Y | I | K | L | O | T | E | G |

NUMBER GAME

| 6 | 5 | 8 | 7 | 8 | 1 | 308 |

CONUNDRUM

| N | I | C | E | G | R | O | U | P |

Round 123

LETTER GAME

1

N	E	T	U	S	T	A	F	E

2

N	U	R	I	S	M	I	V	E

3

A	I	S	T	E	D	S	L	N

NUMBER GAME

50	25	7	2	8	4	**693**

CONUNDRUM

E	N	G	I	N	E	F	U	L

Round 124

LETTER GAME

1 P A T U R A E V F

2 G E S I H T E O N

3 A E F G L O P R Y

NUMBER GAME

| 50 | 8 | 5 | 4 | 9 | 3 | **784** |

CONUNDRUM

R E A L W H I T E

Round 125

LETTER GAME

1

E	F	G	I	N	O	R	V	T

2

A	D	E	I	L	M	N	S	T

3

C	E	I	I	N	O	P	R	S

NUMBER GAME

10	2	10	5	4	6	740

CONUNDRUM

M	A	G	I	C	R	I	N	G

Round 126

LETTER GAME

1
G	X	A	H	E	T	P	N	O

2
E	N	Q	T	U	O	L	P	E

3
S	A	F	M	E	I	D	H	X

NUMBER GAME

100	1	7	9	6	5	248

CONUNDRUM

L	I	T	T	L	E	S	E	A

Round 127

LETTER GAME

1 | A | O | P | L | I | Y | E | L | G |

| | | | | | | | | |

2 | T | G | Y | I | E | D | S | W | A |

| | | | | | | | | |

3 | R | Q | P | I | E | G | T | A | U |

| | | | | | | | | |

NUMBER GAME

| 2 | 8 | 7 | 7 | 5 | 1 | **343** |

CONUNDRUM

| L | A | W | N | G | R | I | P | S |

Round 128

LETTER GAME

1

B	H	E	I	D	O	T	U	R

2

P	R	N	D	E	A	S	O	C

3

N	I	R	U	L	F	I	E	A

NUMBER GAME

75	6	2	4	4	8	555

CONUNDRUM

E	N	O	U	G	H	D	E	T

Competition 8

Richard is often referred to as 'twice _____ Whiteley'.

Round 129

LETTER GAME

1 | C | R | H | R | W | E | A | O | M |

| | | | | | | | | |

2 | N | I | G | Y | E | S | A | V | S |

| | | | | | | | | |

3 | T | V | L | R | I | O | S | M | A |

| | | | | | | | | |

NUMBER GAME

| 50 | 100 | 75 | 3 | 4 | 4 | 659 |

CONUNDRUM

| S | U | M | O | T | R | A | C | Y |

Round 130

LETTER GAME

1

L	T	N	G	E	U	O	D	L

2

P	S	I	O	T	G	A	P	H

3

X	R	T	S	N	E	A	O	Z

NUMBER GAME

25	1	4	1	3	8	622

CONUNDRUM

I	N	T	R	O	A	I	D	A

Round 131

LETTER GAME

1 | F | C | L | D | I | O | E | V | R |

2 | H | R | B | A | T | I | A | T | E |

3 | T | G | S | B | I | A | E | J | L |

NUMBER GAME

| 25 | 50 | 75 | 100 | 9 | 6 | **840** |

CONUNDRUM

| N | U | S | E | N | I | G | H | T |

Round 132

LETTER GAME

1 | D | N | P | U | E | I | K | T | L |

2 | D | P | E | O | H | S | E | G | O |

3 | R | S | W | E | G | O | E | K | N |

NUMBER GAME

| 100 | 10 | 10 | 9 | 9 | 1 | | 629 |

CONUNDRUM

| S | E | M | I | S | T | I | L | L |

Round 133

LETTER GAME

1

C	X	O	A	L	U	R	N	O

2

C	S	E	O	T	H	E	M	F

3

S	T	A	X	U	A	L	D	R

NUMBER GAME

50	3	9	3	9	6	729

CONUNDRUM

S	C	O	T	S	G	E	N	I

Round 134

LETTER GAME

1

D	T	E	I	P	S	E	N	O

2

W	T	M	E	A	I	R	D	S

3

S	T	I	E	U	K	W	O	S

NUMBER GAME

100	7	6	3	2	10	805

CONUNDRUM

N	I	C	E	Q	U	E	S	T

Round 135

LETTER GAME

1

O	L	C	X	S	E	A	O	V

2

M	T	C	N	I	E	O	A	I

3

G	E	R	I	N	D	E	R	A

NUMBER GAME

25	2	5	6	5	3	311

CONUNDRUM

I	D	O	L	S	C	O	U	R

Round 136

LETTER GAME

1

N	H	T	E	I	J	R	E	A

2

C	L	O	E	T	D	I	P	E

3

S	A	N	R	E	L	N	S	A

NUMBER GAME

50	25	6	6	4	4		820

CONUNDRUM

S	I	N	N	E	R	D	O	G

Game 9

Match yourself against ...

David Acton (Series 31 winner)

Round 1   G E P A N I R S N
Round 2   M T E S L O U R Q
Round 3   D E H I T W E L B

Round 4   25 6 3 4 10 7 (166)

Round 5   S M O E V D Y O X
Round 6   T E S I C E F R M
Round 7   H W N A E D L A I

Round 8   25 7 1 2 2 6 (385)

Round 9   MINILUNGS

Round 137

LETTER GAME

1
N	E	S	O	L	C	G	E	Z

2
W	O	I	T	H	R	S	E	E

3
K	A	O	B	D	H	I	T	I

NUMBER GAME

100	10	9	8	2	7	468

CONUNDRUM

S	C	R	U	B	B	I	E	S

Round 138

LETTER GAME

1

M	A	T	Y	V	O	L	N	E

2

A	T	G	R	A	E	K	X	U

3

R	A	N	E	U	H	P	E	T

NUMBER GAME

75	4	6	8	5	5	**795**

CONUNDRUM

I	C	E	S	I	N	N	E	R

Round 139

LETTER GAME

1

N	I	S	D	A	N	V	E	H

2

A	T	H	E	R	T	O	N	S

3

X	I	M	E	N	E	S	D	O

NUMBER GAME

9	6	3	8	2	9	**586**

CONUNDRUM

C	R	A	B	S	W	E	L	L

Round 140

LETTER GAME

1 | G | U | T | T | A | P | O | E | R |

2 | I | M | U | V | N | E | C | A | R |

3 | T | U | E | Q | A | L | S | I | Y |

NUMBER GAME

| 10 | 2 | 6 | 7 | 5 | 1 | **842** |

CONUNDRUM

| P | A | S | T | E | I | G | H | T |

Round 141

LETTER GAME

1

N	O	D	I	F	A	E	T	S

2

A	S	C	E	D	A	C	H	D

3

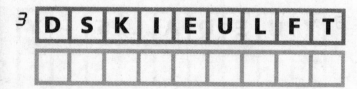

D	S	K	I	E	U	L	F	T

NUMBER GAME

75	8	5	2	9	2	864

CONUNDRUM

T	O	R	Y	D	E	E	D	S

Round 142

LETTER GAME

1

R	D	G	O	E	V	A	R	P

2

D	M	S	M	E	I	A	S	L

3

P	D	T	I	E	A	N	T	L

NUMBER GAME

100	6	8	4	1	1	**526**

CONUNDRUM

G	I	A	N	T	B	E	R	T

Round 143

LETTER GAME

1

L	R	G	O	E	O	S	N	C

2

S	N	W	O	I	A	T	P	U

3

R	Y	R	A	I	A	B	L	S

NUMBER GAME

25	4	3	3	1	2	923

CONUNDRUM

E	N	T	E	R	H	E	A	D

LETTER GAME

1

L	X	P	E	A	E	F	H	M

2

R	C	T	M	A	I	E	G	D

3

T	N	L	E	A	E	S	T	K

NUMBER GAME

25	9	10	8	2	2	781

CONUNDRUM

M	I	N	E	R	B	U	N	G

Competition 9

What nationality is tennis ace Vijay Amritraj, who appeared in Dictionary Corner in 1999?

Round 145

LETTER GAME

1

B	G	F	A	O	I	E	R	T

2

S	P	O	I	G	M	E	O	B

3

F	I	U	I	G	L	S	E	T

NUMBER GAME

75	4	3	5	4	1	860

CONUNDRUM

S	T	E	V	E	D	A	T	A

Round 146

LETTER GAME

1

S	U	E	T	Y	O	I	S	L

2

Q	I	U	A	E	R	F	G	H

3

U	R	D	B	I	S	L	E	G

NUMBER GAME

50	8	7	5	3	2	916

CONUNDRUM

T	A	R	T	I	R	U	B	Y

Round 147

LETTER GAME

1 | N | D | E | A | M | L | I | C | E |

| | | | | | | | | |

2 | D | T | I | N | O | M | A | N | E |

| | | | | | | | | |

3 | L | A | S | T | E | L | I | T | E |

| | | | | | | | | |

NUMBER GAME

| 25 | 7 | 4 | 1 | 7 | 4 | **465** |

CONUNDRUM

| D | U | N | N | I | G | R | O | G |

Round 148

LETTER GAME

1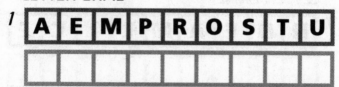

A E M P R O S T U

2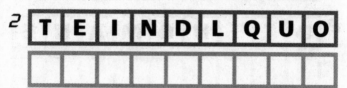

T E I N D L Q U O

3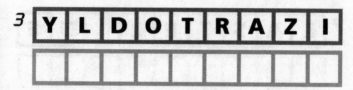

Y L D O T R A Z I

NUMBER GAME

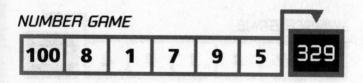

| 100 | 8 | 1 | 7 | 9 | 5 | 329 |

CONUNDRUM

L A B N U T T E R

Round 149

LETTER GAME

1

R	A	I	R	E	B	L	Y	Z

2

U	P	T	H	E	N	O	S	E

3

R	S	T	O	I	D	E	W	U

NUMBER GAME

100	75	3	3	4	6	849

CONUNDRUM

G	O	L	D	N	M	I	L	E

Round 150

LETTER GAME

1

P	O	R	A	C	E	T	O	V

2

Z	D	P	I	O	M	T	E	H

3

N	L	X	O	A	S	T	O	I

NUMBER GAME

25	3	7	10	5	6	624

CONUNDRUM

M	A	L	E	T	U	N	I	C

Round 151

LETTER GAME

1 | L | R | M | E | O | T | N | I | V |

2 | T | A | N | O | V | U | G | T | E |

3 | S | A | E | N | T | M | I | N | G |

NUMBER GAME

| 4 | 9 | 8 | 8 | 2 | 1 | | 650 |

CONUNDRUM

| G | R | A | C | E | R | U | S | H |

Round 152

LETTER GAME

1

X	A	T	G	A	L	H	E	W

2

O	I	S	N	V	A	D	E	H

3

L	A	M	T	E	Y	T	I	S

NUMBER GAME

50	7	3	6	9	5	988

CONUNDRUM

N	E	V	E	R	W	I	T	I

Game 10

Match yourself against ...

Wayne Summers (Series 24 winner)

Round 1	S B G E A V J I S
Round 2	D M E A R T L I G
Round 3	H T N U I Q R A E
Round 4	10 3 3 10 4 9 (100)
Round 5	P V N O E L R A D
Round 6	S W I E N R O C G
Round 7	R S D A E I M G N
Round 8	25 3 2 5 6 8 5 (743)
Round 9	GIANTMULE

Round 153

LETTER GAME

1

N	T	Z	O	A	I	P	R	E

2

B	O	J	E	D	G	A	N	A

3

A	C	E	E	H	I	L	V	R

NUMBER GAME

75	7	5	1	1	3	666

CONUNDRUM

C	O	S	Y	D	I	V	E	R

Round 154

LETTER GAME

1 | A | B | E | I | J | N | O | R | W |

2 | A | C | E | F | L | O | N | R | Y |

3 | S | T | E | U | P | E | A | L | C |

NUMBER GAME

| 50 | 6 | 1 | 3 | 5 | 4 | | 876 |

CONUNDRUM

| S | U | P | E | R | C | H | A | D |

Round 155

LETTER GAME

1

O	O	T	H	P	A	S	T	E

2

E	H	I	O	P	S	U	R	V

3

C	E	E	E	G	I	N	R	T

NUMBER GAME

50	7	2	8	9	1	875

CONUNDRUM

T	R	I	P	L	E	B	U	N

Round 156

LETTER GAME

1

A	D	E	I	L	M	T	T	U

2

H	A	G	N	I	B	E	D	E

3

L	E	D	S	A	R	B	O	U

NUMBER GAME

7	6	10	2	2	1	**524**

CONUNDRUM

R	E	D	S	I	P	P	E	R

Round 157

LETTER GAME

1 | M | N | O | T | P | L | R | E | A |

2 | D | A | L | L | I | S | E | W | K |

3 | Z | E | R | T | I | L | S | E | I |

NUMBER GAME

| 25 | 3 | 8 | 8 | 1 | 6 | **555** |

CONUNDRUM

| F | I | C | K | L | E | R | O | D |

Round 158

LETTER GAME

1 L E T O M G I R O

2 P N I E L D C K U

3 H L O P E S T O S

NUMBER GAME

| 75 | 2 | 9 | 1 | 5 | 10 | 833 |

CONUNDRUM

G R E E N L A D Y

Round 159

LETTER GAME

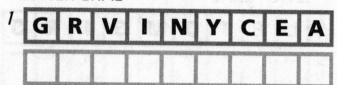
1. G R V I N Y C E A

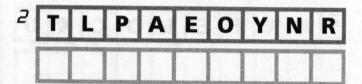
2. T L P A E O Y N R

3. T Y A U E L S H V

NUMBER GAME

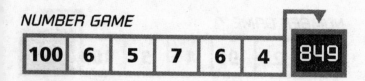
| 100 | 6 | 5 | 7 | 6 | 4 | **849** |

CONUNDRUM

N I G H T W O R D

Round 160

LETTER GAME

1 | J | E | N | I | O | S | G | L | S |

2 | C | C | E | E | N | D | O | R | S |

3 | A | L | I | M | R | O | S | T | U |

NUMBER GAME

| 50 | 25 | 100 | 4 | 1 | 8 | **676** |

CONUNDRUM

| N | I | G | H | T | W | I | R | E |

Answers

Round 1
UNIXERTAN   taurine (7) tanner (6) annex (5)
GIEDVISCS   viscid (6) discs (5) vied (4)
ETOXHNOGU   touching (8) toughen (7) enough (6)

$7 \times 5 = 35$; $35 \times 25 = 875$; $875 + 9 + 3 = 887$

DISTURBED

Round 2
LRKCAEEMF   mackerel (8) freckle (7) remake (6)
FADIOGERN   organdie (8) reading (7) fringe (6)
BRISHENDA   brandish (8) handier (7) brains (6)

$3 \times 2 \times 25 = 150$; $150 - (4 + 4) = 142$; $142 \times 6 = 852$

PROVOKING

Round 3
OEWMNOFRG   frogmen (7) woofer (6) frown (5)
NREYABTON   bayonet (7) banner (6) abort (5)
RDGEAETBT   battered (8) rebated (7) target (6)

$(3 \times 3) \times (50 + 25) = 675$; $675 - (6 + 2) = 667$

HEALTHIER

Round 4
ERDMINAOZ   randomize (9) romanize (8) aneroid (7)
RINGCOWEL   lowering (8) cowgirl (7) winger (6)
JAEDIETNC   injected (8) jadeite (7) decant (6)

$75 + 4 + 1 = 80$; $80 \times 9 = 720$

LEATHERED

Round 5
TLARKEENM   telemark (8) eternal (7) market (6)
NUTNFIAEO   fountain (8) tonneau (7) infant (6)
BEIHSTOIV   bothies (7) soviet (6) visit (5)

$(8 \times 25) + 6 = 206$; $206 \times 4 = 824$

YESTERDAY

Round 6

KIHADEVSE	adhesive (8) heavies (7) devise (6)
OBLADIMYC	amyloid (7) cymbal (6) madly (5)
QUSEIDLFI	fluidise (8) liquids (7) fields (6)

$(9 + 8) \times 25 = 425$; $425 - 6 = 419$; $419 \times (1 + 1) = 838$

SPARKLING

Round 7

GYOOBRIEN	obeying (7) ignore (6) being (5)
SCUORABIL	caribous (8) carious (7) social (6)
GNJOISNAC	consign (7) casino (6) joins (5)

$7 + 2 + 2 = 11$; $11 + (4 \times 25) = 111$; $111 \times 8 = 888$

AWARENESS

Round 8

HUBEASRDN	husbander (9) unshared (8) brushed (7)
NLEUCAREL	nucellar (8) nuclear (7) recall (6)
DCINDORER	cornier (7) coined (6) décor (5)

$(10 - 8) \times 100 = 200$; $(8 \times 7) - 10 = 46$; $200 + 46 = 246$

CATHEDRAL

Round 9

ISTAFEMNO	manifesto (9) amniotes (8) moisten (7)
HOCUSAIGN	housing (8) anguish (7) chains (6)
HBIEISVTN	invites (7) invest (6) thine (5)

$6 \times (25 - 2) = 138$; $138 - 4 = 134$; $134 \times 5 = 670$; $670 - 1 = 669$

IMPRESSED

Round 10

OCDUYELRV	crudely (7) clover (6) cloud (5)
SENAGLIMG	gleaming (8) niggles (7) mangle (6)
EASSMITRF	misrates (8) firmest (7) stairs (6)

$5 \times (100 + 50) = 750$; $4 + 2 = 6$; $6/6 = 1$; $750 - 1 = 749$

PROCESSOR

Round 11

PYSTALIOC	capitols (8) optical (7) policy (6)
VCESOTENA	centavos (8) octaves (7) encase (6)
AIGDLAEPW	dewlap (6) agile (5) wade (4)

$(3 \times 25) - 1 = 74$; $74 \times 9 = 666$

SLAPSTICK

Round 12

NHNIARMEK	ramekin (7) remain (6) hiker (5)
NEEOXYTAG	oxygenate (9) goatee (6) tango (5)
ETRUBTMSA	maturest (8) smatter (7) breast (6)

$(10 + 8) \times 50 = 900$; $100/4 = 25$; $900 + 25 = 925$

AEROPLANE

Round 13

TGIANRUYA	guaranty (8) unitary (7) grainy (6)
HLVRAOEMT	removal (7) mother (6) lover (5)
SCNKIUMET	muckiest (8) minuets (7) musket (6)

$100 + 75 - 2 = 173; 173 \times 4 = 692$

UPSTAGING

Round 14

VRFGOILDE	frivoled (8) forgive (7) lodger (6)
LSGOUDIRE	guilders (8) groused (7) soured (6)
MTOASBERN	monstera (8) batsmen (7) ornate (6)

$100 - 5 = 95; (7 + 3) \times 95 = 950; 950 - 4 = 946$

MATCHLESS

Round 15

UDLFROWEP	powerful (8) floured (7) poured (6)
FPNAYOLME	maypole (7) eponym (6) flame (5)
AITENDUQA	antiqued (8) audient (7) detain (6)

$50 + (75/25) = 53; 8 + 2 = 10; 53 \times 10 = 530$

TEMPERING

Round 16

WPODLETZA	waltzed (7) zealot (6) delta (5)
RSRMEOAPT	rearmost (8) stamper (7) poster (6)
GREALWAYD	already (7) lawyer (6) grade (5)

$9 + 5 = 14; 25 + 8 = 33; 14 \times 33 = 462; 462 + 7 = 469$

MEDITATED

Round 17

EFGHILWTY	flyweight (9) whitefly (8) weighty (7)
OKRYBANDE	keyboard (8) broaden (7) brandy (6)
LBEYSATRE	easterly (8) trebles (7) rebate (6)

$3 \times (2 + 1) = 9; 100 + 2 + 1 = 103; 9 \times 103 = 927$

DISPERSED

Round 18

NSMEUCOEP	consume (7) pounce (6) scone (5)
NRLUEOYSD	roundels (8) soundly (7) yonder (6)
BEUFGIRQT	briquet (7) figure (6) quiet (5)

$(8 \times 100) - 75 = 725; 725 - 6 = 719$

BRIEFCASE

Round 19

RULPDIAVE	epidural (8) prevail (7) repaid (6)
JHENBLIOT	hotline (7) bothie (6) thine (5)
PGSNPOTEA	stoppage (8) stopgap (7) sponge (6)

$(7 - 1) \times 6 = 36; 36 \times 8 = 288$

INTERFERE

Round 20

ELIMNANYV naively (7) menial (6) anvil (5)
HMOEOISNF moonfish (8) noisome (7) monies (6)
SIPOTCHLI politics (8) solicit (7) pistol (6)

$3 \times (75/25) = 9; 9 \times 50 = 450; 450 + 100 + 4 = 554$

JOURNEYED

Round 21

LSBTNUIED insulted (8) dustbin (7) blinds (6)
CTXWEIEOR exoteric (8) coterie (7) excite (6)
SUBADORIN dinosaur (8) ordains (7) bounds (6)

$(5 - 3) \times 50 = 100; (100 + 8) \times (8 - 1) = 756$

HAMPERING

Round 22

GBRSIEFUG firebugs (8) figures (7) bigger (6)
HENOWSBIT wishbone (8) townies (7) bestow (6)
TUDOGERAS outraged (8) groused (7) stored (6)

$(6 + 4) \times 50 = 500; 500 - (9 + 8) = 483$

OTHERWISE

Round 23

WRACBEULG curable (7) warble (6) crawl (5)
NSRCEIWEY scenery (7) winery (6) crews (5)
LAMBORDIE bromeliad (9) rambled (7) ordeal (6)

$(10 \times 25) - 2 = 248; 9 - 5 = 4; 248 \times 4 = 992$

CONJURING

Round 24

AJREBOWTO rowboat (7) booter (6) orate (5)
TMIEDAFIW midwife (7) dimwit (6) media (5)
EYORLIPAT polarity (8) topiary (7) pirate (6)

$7 - (8 - 7) = 6; (6 \times 100) - 4 = 596$

BREAKFAST

Round 25

JOTWANSEB jawbones (8) banjoes (7) absent (6)
DBEATSLUW sublated (8) bustled (7) wasted (6)
AHMURNEEJ humaner (7) rename (6) harem (5)

$(3 \times 5) + 1 = 16; 16 \times 50 = 800; 800 + 4 - 3 = 801$

SPIRALLED

Round 26

ODRYURSVE surveyor (8) devours (7) drover (6)
AITHKRCSO chariots (8) haricot (7) charts (6)
SHSRWIOAT trishaws (8) wraiths (7) assort (6)

$(6 \times 75) - (7 \times 5) = 415; 415 + (50/25) = 417$

HORSEBACK

183

Round 27

ASCTORVRE   overcast (8) avocets (7) carrot (6)
YLINPRTEA   interplay (9) triplane (8) painter (7)
POINDRGAS   poniards (8) draping (7) pianos (6)

$(6 - 2) \times (75 + 10) = 340; \quad 340 + 7 = 347$

NEWSPAPER

Round 28

AMIUMEDSL   dilemmas (8) mislead (7) medium (6)
GAIRMYEST   migrates (8) mastery (7) armies (6)
MLCEINOXA   exclaim (7) climax (6) camel (5)

$5 \times 6 \times 3 \times 3 = 270; \quad 270 + 4/4 = 271$

FRUMPIEST

Round 29

RSOMAETBD   broadest (8) boasted (7) master (6)
KLDYTEAEC   lackeyed (8) tackled (7) tacked (6)
CEIDPRQUE   pedicure (8) pierced (7) piqued (6)

$(5 \times 5) + 10 = 35; \quad 35 \times 25 = 875; \quad 875 - (10 + 1) = 864$

HOLIDAYED

Round 30

FYSZEUIPT   stupefy (7) putzes (6) piety (5)
CSNAEOPLA   palaces (7) canoes (6) place (5)
RIPTCUSER   scripture (9) pictures (8) curries (7)

$5 \times (25 + 3) = 140; \quad 140 \times 7 = 980$

CIVILISED

Round 31

TAREPOCHN   chaperon (8) another (7) trance (6)
TSLEAIBOP   epiblast (8) potable (7) albeit (6)
SDUETZYOW   stowed (6) dusty (5) dozy (4)

$100 - (7 \times 4) = 72; \quad 72 \times 8 = 576; \quad 576 - 2 = 574$

ADVENTURE

Round 32

REDRITGFU   drifter (7) fidget (6) fruit (5)
NEVIOLBOI   oblivion (8) olivine (7) violin (6)
TGHOESASH   hostages (8) sheaths (7) ghost (6)

$75 + 5 = 80; \quad 80 \times (8 + 4) = 960; \quad 960 - 9 = 951$

GAMBOLLED

Round 33

PAORTXHSE   thoraxes (8) earshot (7) hoaxes (6)
ESYTALCNR   ancestry (8) crystal (7) traces (6)
VRIEILMNF   filmier (7) virile (6) flier (5)

$7 \times (75 + 25) = 700; \quad 50 - (9 + 6) = 35; \quad 700 - 35 = 665$

POCKETING

Round 34

MGWLIODEA   miaowed (7) mildew (6) gleam (5)
TESODGTAS   toasted (7) seadog (6) goats (5)
EDIMLCTEA   decimate (8) dialect (7) malted (6)

$(10 + 9) \times 4 = 76; 76 \times (5 \times 2) = 760$

DASTARDLY

Round 35

DAILEIFNZ   finalized (9) infidel (7) finale (6)
GRYORUAPT   purgatory (9) portray (7) yogurt (6)
SPBAUOMGS   possum (6) spasm (5) gasp (4)

$7 \times 7 \times 3 = 147; 147 + (5/5) = 148; 148 \times 3 = 444$

HUMILIATE

Round 36

AYEFDPRMI   firedamp(8) pyramid (7) dreamy (6)
ABDILOVTE   violated (8) tabloid (7) bolted (6)
DEURTOGRS   drugstore (9) grouters (8) rousted (7)

$6 + 5 + 4 = 15; 15 \times 25 = 375; 375 + 8 = 383$

RENDITION

Round 37

RTOPCBLAI   tropical (8) parboil (7) coital (6)
TYPOSTREA   tapestry (8) teapots (7) sporty (6)
LKYOOASCP   calypso (7) cloaks (6) spool (5)

$10 + 1 - 4 = 7; (100 + 6) \times 7 = 742; 742 + 5 = 747$

COMMUNION

Round 38

GETODARDE   derogated (9) degrade (7) goatee (6)
FBUIOLTRA   orbital (7) artful (6) ultra (5)
HLGAEITLN   atheling (8) gelatin (7) alight (6)

$50 + (9 \times 4) = 86; 86 \times 7 = 602$

PRIVILEGE

Round 39

DYLHITSOA   holidays (8) hastily (7) stolid (6)
OFSGIXDEH   dogfish (7) oxhide (6) hosed (5)
BGAOSZPEA   gazebos (7) seabag (6) pages (5)

$(9 \times 25) + 6 + 3 = 234; 234 \times 4 = 936; 936 + 2 = 938$

REPAIRING

Round 40

SUEQYBRAL   squarely (8) equably (7) barley (6)
EDHLEATFI   deflate (7) failed (6) hated (5)
TRIDANKWE   knitwear (8) tawnier (7) winked (6)

$25 + 6 - 1 = 30; 9 + 7 = 16; 30 \times 16 = 480; 480 - 2 = 478$

CONCEALED

Round 41

LLWOESIRT   lowliest (8) toilers (7) writes (6)
FTWEOESLN   oneself (7) lowest (6) fleet (5)
LPUEETIDN   plenitude (9) detinue (7) pelted (6)

$3 \times (3 + 4) = 21$; $21 \times 25 = 525$; $525 + 8 - 6 = 527$

BELITTLED

Round 42

ADACWKRBE   drawback (8) wracked (7) arcade (6)
DCRASPIEP   scrapped (8) sidecar (7) aspire (6)
NOGNISEAD   diagnose (8) agonise (7) seadog (6)

$(75 + 3) \times (5 + 4) = 702$; $702 + 2 = 704$

ADDICTION

Round 43

APDLUARGE   upgrade (7) laager (6) purge (5)
RSBIOTDEO   broodiest (9) steroid (7) booted (6)
VTEAMULAF   valuate (7) amulet (6) vault (5)

$100 - 3 = 97$; $(8 + 2) \times 97 = 970$; $970 - 4 = 966$

BELIEVING

Round 44

GROWILMAN   roaming (7) lowing (6) groan (5)
ACHIDNETS   distance (8) chained (7) hinted (6)
BIRDEHMIS   dishier (7) brides (6) hired (5)

$10 \times (5 + 5) = 100$; $(100 + 7) \times (6 + 3) = 963$

STIPULATE

Round 45

CPBRYEIER   piercer (7) creepy (6) price (5)
RMDAOTVEA   matador (7) dreamt (6) avert (5)
SNODIFAGH   dogfish (7) gonads (6) gnash (5)

$(9 + 4) \times 25 = 325$; $325 + 6 + 2 = 333$

UNIVERSAL

Round 46

COBRELOEH   borehole (8) belcher (7) breech (6)
FADEGTOPO   footage (7) goofed (6) adopt (5)
GTIOXEASC   geotaxis (8) exotica (7) ageist (6)

$6 \times 50 = 300$; $25 \times 3 = 75$; $300 - (75/75) = 299$

FLUCTUATE

Round 47

DOSRIWOND   indoors (7) disown (6) drown (5)
FALRYUPEI   failure (7) purify (6) flare (5)
TPNIUOATS   pantsuit (8) outspan (7) pianos (6)

$2 \times (4 + 1) = 10$; $10 \times (100 - 4) = 960$

DISPUTING

Round 48

SUOLVICES   coulisse (8) viscose (7) sluice (6)
GORVITAND   graviton (8) adoring (7) virago (6)
DRAOBGITN   boarding (8) dingbat (7) adroit (6)

$7 + 5 - 1 = 11; 3 \times 11 = 33; 9 \times 75 = 675; 675 - 33 = 642$

IMBALANCE

Round 49

OSCHAZEPY   poaches (7) psycho (6) space (5)
GMRAENCOH   echogram (8) monarch (7) chrome (6)
TIARJCOSA   caritas (7) racist (6) actor (5)

$8 \times (9 + 2) = 88; 9 \times (88 - 5) = 747; 747 + 1 = 748$

CARTWHEEL

Round 50

BTAACLEHE   teachable (9) heatable (8) actable (7)
ELTDTEERA   lettered (8) related (7) dealer (6)
OEINBVHAG   behaving (8) begonia (7) hoeing (6)

$50 + 9 - 8 = 51; 51 \times 7 = 357; 357 - (10/10) = 356$

DEVOURING

Round 51

YBGFAAUER   argufy (6) rugby (5) beau (4)
SMTESPUDI   disputes (8) stumped (7) upsets (6)
OMLARTIUS   simulator (9) moralist (8) outsail (7)

$(75 - 1) \times 2 = 148; 148 \times 2 = 296; 296 - 6 = 290$

BALLISTIC

Round 52

NIERTHWAG   nightwear (9) watering (8) hairnet (7)
ADFEINRDR   infrared (8) randier (7) friend (6)
NREYABTON   bayonet (7) notary (6) entry (5)

$(6 \times 6) - 2 = 34; \ 25 - 2 = 23; 34 \times 23 = 782; 782 + 3 = 785$

FOREFRONT

Round 53

NGTEAOBIJ   begonia (7) obtain (6) jingo (5)
RDGEAETVT   targeted (8) averted (7) vetted (6)
KTUESLEGY   sleeky (6) lutes (5) luke (4)

$50 - 1 = 49; (3 \times 5) - 1 = 14; 49 \times 14 = 686$

SURPASSED

Round 54

JNSUACENT   nutcase (7) jaunts (6) scant (5)
GRIEANWNE   renewing (8) warning (7) regain (6)
BTYRIISCA   sybaritic (9) basicity (8) satiric (7)

$9 \times 7 = 63; 63 \times (10 - 2) = 504; 504 - 100 = 404$

PROTRUDED

Round 55

EHEILDANW   headline (8) inhaled (7) wailed (6)
RONETJUIP   eruption (8) juniper (7) punter (6)
OBSLAEMRC   scramble (8) oracles (7) carols (6)

$6 \times 5 \times 2 \times 2 = 120; 120 - 7 = 113; 113 \times 8 = 904$

LOCALISED

Round 56

PLGODIAUE   dialogue (8) plagued (7) lapdog (6)
ANYIVTELO   natively (8) violent (7) litany (6)
SOAVGEISE   visages (7) sieges (6) visas (5)

$75 + 8 - 5 = 78; (78 \times 10) - 1 = 779$

WEAKENING

Round 57

TSOEACJNI   canoeist (8) jaconet (7) action (6)
KATJEATDN   attend (6) naked (5) data (4)
EBHAMONDR   hornbeam (8) abdomen (7) moaner (6)

$(2 \times 9) + 1 = 19; 19 \times 25 = 475; 475 - (10 + 3) = 462$

GLAMOROUS

Round 58

BIMONALMA   ammonia (7) animal (6) mania (5)
LEGASNYIC   saliency (8) angelic (7) nicely (6)
NAPEJROYL   plenary (7) japery (6) prone (5)

$8 \times (100 - 10) = 720; 720 - 3 - 1 = 716$

APPEARING

Round 59

LIMAHIGSR   similar (7) garish (6) rails (5)
KSUPGAODE   padouks (7) soaked (6) spoke (5)
EDGIOTYED   oddity (6) doted (5) edge (4)

$(2 \times 5) + 3 = 13; 75 + 13 = 88; 88 \times 8 = 704$

TRADITION

Round 60

UPNTIAKDO   opuntia (7) kidnap (6) point (5)
ZIUENXASD   unsized (7) unisex (6) sedan (50
QSBOIATRU   quartos (7) robust (6) bouts (5)

$50 - 3 = 47; 10 + 10 + 5 - 4 = 21; 47 \times 21 = 987$

ELEGANTLY

Round 61

FGROIESHL   golfers (7) sleigh (6) rifle (5)
YVUSDIENT   density (7) nudity (6) vines (5)
WNTUONARE   neutron (7) wanton (6) owner (5)

$9 - (50/25) = 7; 100 - (6/6) = 99; 7 \times 99 = 693$

STUPEFIED

Round 62

AVTIREDLU	durative (8) virtual (7) valued (6)
SNEAGLMIG	gleaming (8) niggles (7) silage (6)
NGTRCAOBI	botanic (7) racing (6) organ (5)

$(5 + 3) \times 75 = 600$; $9 \times (7 - 4) = 27$; $600 - 27 = 573$

DORMITORY

Round 63

EASSMITRF	smarties (8) firmest (7) fiesta (6)
IERFBTOSE	briefest (8) forties (7) fibres (6)
BGEIRDSUP	bruised (7) superb (6) grubs (5)

$50 + 7 - 6 = 51$; $8 + 8 + 1 = 17$; $17 \times 51 = 867$

POTENTIAL

Round 64

NDEAMLIWR	mineral (7) wailed (6) dream (5)
NOINITFGY	notifying (9) toying (6) ingot (5)
EIMNQSTUY	mystique (8) minuets (7) squint (6)

$9 \times 50 = 450$; $450 + 25 - 3 = 472$; $472 \times 2 = 944$

COMFORTED

Round 65

YACDGTERO	category (8) cordage (7) graced (6)
ACEEIFNRT	interface (9) frenetic (8) fiancee (7)
ULTRALIBY	brutally (8) tilbury (7) burial (6)

$(100 + 75) \times 5 = 875 + 10 = 885$

REQUISITE

Round 66

GIFATOUER	fruitage (8) outrage (7) figure (6)
GHSIUOLFK	folkish (7) ghouls (6) flogs (5)
DZEOIOPES	episode (7) seized (6) posed (5)

$75 + 25 + 8 - 3 = 105$; $105 \times 9 = 945$

IRRITATED

Round 67

CSINARPEN	crannies (8) spanner (7) cranes (6)
MARTYORNE	monetary (8) anymore (7) ornate (6)
HISVEROTL	hostile (7) violet (6) stole (5)

$8 + 6 + 3 = 17$; $50 + 1 = 51$; $17 \times 51 = 867$

PROLONGED

Round 68

TLRIEGMAR	armiger (7) retail (6) grime (5)
HINSAGLOT	loathing (8) salting (7) gloats (6)
BERYTUNAC	cybernaut (9) century (7) butane (6)

$5 \times (4 + 1) = 25$; $25 \times 25 = 625$; $625 + 10 - 7 = 628$

SPECIALTY

Round 69

SARTOESKB	boasters (8) baskets (7) sorbet (6)
NBNEAILPS	biplanes (8) lesbian (7) saline (6)
EAIBYTRNH	hairnet (7) brainy (6) habit (5)

$10 \times (9 + 7) = 160$; $8 \times 7 = 56$; $160 + 56 = 216$; $216 + 10 = 226$

HARROWING

Round 70

GJLEAISDF	gadflies (8) ladies (6) field (5)
PRADOTATE	tetrapod (8) rotated (7) potter (6)
URVILETOR	ulterior (8) outlive (7) revolt (6)

$(7 - 1) \times 100 = 600$; $9 \times (4 + 1) = 45$; $600 - 45 = 555$

POLLUTING

Round 71

TIMLOPEDS	implodes (8) mildest (7) posted (6)
LKTAEPRAC	placate (7) packer (6) creak (5)
SPOIHNECA	canopies (8) pinches (7) chains (6)

$3 \times (2 + 1) = 9$; $9 \times 4 \times 3 = 108$; $108 \times 8 = 864$

SCHOOLBOY

Round 72

NGHEIEDTN	thinned (7) engine (6) thing (5)
TSVNOIUDA	astound (7) divots (6) vaunt (5)
OATFBNKUG	gunboat (7) nougat (6) about (5)

$(2 \times 3) + 1 = 7$; $7 \times 6 \times 5 \times 4 = 840$

MATERNITY

Round 73

GZNUEASLD	unglazed (8) dangles (7) sludge (6)
ALBOTEREI	liberate (8) bloater (7) rebate (6)
FOGAHOYRL	loofah (6) royal (5) yoga (4)

$100 - 7 = 93$; $93 \times 2 \times 2 = 372$

CLASSICAL

Round 74

ENVUIJSKR	junkies (7) injure (6) virus (5)
EOEBNTYAG	bayonet (7) goatee (6) agent (5)
SREOMMETI	memories (8) moister (7) simmer (6)

$(10 + 7) \times 50 = 850$; $(2 \times 6) + 9 = 21$; $850 + 21 = 871$

ABSCONDED

Round 75

NLREUSGWA	granules (8) wrangle (7) lagers (6)
BOPDANGIR	boarding (8) adoring (7) dragon (6)
GRAFICBEN	refacing (8) carbine (7) finger (6)

$4 \times (100 + 50) = 600$; $9 - (75/25) = 6$; $600 + 6 = 606$

FLATTERED

Round 76

  OSTEYRABU   saboteur (8) boaters (7) beauty (6)
  SBIASTOUS   bassist (7) boasts (6) autos (5)
  AELIGSACL   glacial (7) allies (6) glace (5)
  (4 x 7) + 4 = 32; 32 x 25 = 800; 800 + 10 + 2 = 812
  SOMETHING

Round 77

  CREIDOLVY   viceroy (7) drivel (6) cover (5)
  CMSAEOGUL   cagoules (8) glucose (7) solace (6)
  WERIHCEBX   chewier (7) breech (6) where (5)
  8 x (50 − 9) = 328; 328 − 10 − 7 = 311
  SEMAPHORE

Round 78

  LRNOUEYSF   yourself (8) ourself (7) surely (6)
  RNATGODCE cartoned (8) redcoat (7) traced (6)
  LSGIAEPTN   elapsing (8) slating (7) planet (6)
  9 + 6 = 15; 25 − 2 = 23; 15 x 23 = 345; 345 + 1 + 1 = 347
  PLOUGHMAN

Round 79

  BSUXRELHA   blusher (7) herbal (6) relax (5)
  AACDEILLN   dalliance (9) alliance (8) cedilla (7)
  CEILNOQUX   equinox (7) clique (6) quoin (5)
  (10 + 8) x 50 = 900; (5 x 8) − 7 = 33; 900 + 33 = 933
  BENEFITED

Round 80

  BEIORSTUV   obtrusive (9) vitreous (8) bustier (7)
  OCATGEHPD poached (7) coated (6) phage (5)
  VERHENFIG   fevering (8) freeing (7) heifer (6)
  4 x (10 − 1) = 36; (36 − 1) x 25 = 875
  CONGEALED

Round 81

  ASKROLYCI   croakily (8) scarily (7) cloaks (6)
  LRZLUEIGY   uglier (6) gruel (5) rely (4)
  RNQOAUCSI coquina (7) cousin (6) incur (5)
  2 x (50 + 1) = 102; 102 + 75 + 9 = 186
  TESTIMONY

Round 82

  LGAIPSARB   argalis (7) spiral (6) sprig (5)
  LRZOAERMT relator (7) zealot (6) alter (5)
  AIONRYTCV   voracity (8) victory (7) crayon (6)
  10 x (9 + 8) = 170; 170 + 75 = 245; 245 − (9 − 8) = 244
  DEHYDRATE

Round 83
OEITFSXAD   fixated (7) fiesta (6) taxes (5)
GDCIAEOTB   iceboat (7) coated (6) debit (5)
THMULUORF   mouthful (8) hurtful (7) fourth (6)
$9 \times 8 = 72$; $10 - 2 = 8$; $(72 + 1) \times 8 = 584$
FASCINATE

Round 84
AYDEIOVPL   vapidly (7) deploy (6) yield (5)
YHMTPUIDE   thumped (7) tedium (6) thyme (5)
ERPIMTCEF   imperfect (9) receipt (7) temper (6)
$(25 + 2) \times 10 = 270$; $(270 + 4) \times 2 = 548$; $548 + 7 = 555$
SMOOTHING

Round 85
SFRLHOUIE   flourish (8) ourself (7) relish (6)
TRTIEIDVD   divider (7) divert (6) tired (5)
SGACOSITD   dacoits (7) coasts (6) stoic (5)
$7 \times (4 + 3) = 49$; $49 \times 6 = 294$
HANDIWORK

Round 86
HUDOEENDT   denoted (7) hunted (6) ended (5)
FLACDIEYL   facilely (8) ideally (7) filled (6)
OESFTIDSU   outsides (8) softies (7) tissue (6)
$100 - (10/5) = 98$; $98 \times 7 = 686$; $686 - 50 + 3 = 639$
CONSONANT

Round 87
GRTADISES   disaster (8) tigress (7) stairs (6)
CELEDATAS   escalated (9) escalade (8) delates (7)
RUTYOIPAL   polarity (8) outplay (7) parity (6)
$(75/25) \times 100 = 300$; $300 + 50 + 2 = 352$; $352 \times 2 = 704$
ASTOUNDED

Round 88
OGHAITLRS   alright (7) sailor (6) light (5)
DRAIWIGNP   pairing (7) inward (6) wring (5)
BMOAGNERO   boomerang (9) oregano (7) maroon (6)
$100 - (2 \times 10) = 80$; $6 \times 80 = 480$; $480 - 9 = 471$
SUFFOCATE

Round 89
NOSIHOARU   nourish (7) onrush (6) shorn (5)
DCUEWSOID   discoed (7) escudo (6) diced (5)
RSCAOATPI   apricots (8) captors (7) script (6)
$6 - (1 + 1) = 4$; $4 \times (50 + 8) = 232$; $232 + 7 = 239$
CONTINENT

Round 90
LEPSEZRIY	replies (7) eerily (6) prize (5)
PELIMTURC	plectrum (8) crumpet (7) triple (6)
OSIRCOEVR	corrosive (9) corries (7) voices (6)

(9 – 4) x (100 + 2) = 510; 510 + 75 = 585; 585 – 7 = 578

PROTESTED

Round 91
ALUTOAVEN	ovulate (7) volant (6) naval (5)
NAROFYLEP	profanely (9) foreplay (8) palfrey (7)
ELUIVONSA	avulsion (8) unveils (7) saline (6)

(8 x 75) + 25 = 625; 625 – (6/3) = 623

POPULATED

Round 92
LWODSLIOE	woollies (8) swilled (7) slowed (6)
EIGYUDRHS	greyish (7) rushed (6) hides (5)
CNOCATOUP	occupant (8) coconut (7) toucan (6)

(7 x 25) + 7 = 182; 182 x 5 = 910; 910 + (8/2) = 914

AUTOGRAPH

Round 93
ADDEGINOS	diagnosed (9) adenoids (8) agonies (7)
DDUUNRSEE	underused (9) sundered (8) endured (7)
RTAGESHOS	shortages (9) hostages (8) earshot (7)

9 x (100 – 9) = 819; 6 + (2/2) = 7; 819 + 7 = 826

GRIEVANCE

Round 94
YDGIEIRNO	ignored (7) indigo (6) irony (5)
UEARDWVLO	roulade (7) valour (6) drove (5)
EHIORSTWZ	howitzers (9) worthies (8) zithers (7)

(4 x 10) – 3 = 37; 37 x 25 = 925; 925 + 7 + 5 = 937

EXPOUNDED

Round 95
EIJNOSSTT	jettisons (9) stoniest (8) nosiest (7)
ACEIIMRST	armistice (9) scimitar (8) airtime (7)
LERHOEWYN	nowhere (7) howler (6) owner (5)

(9 + 7) x 9 = 144

INTEGRITY

Round 96
VATPECALO	polecat (7) octave (6) clove (5)
DSEOGXNEP	expends (7) sponge (6) dopes (5)
EVADBLITR	vibrated (8) trailed (7) braved (6)

100 + 75 + 50 + 25 = 250; 250 – 3 = 247; 247 x 3 = 741

DIFFERING

Round 97
TDNIUIMLO   dilution (8) untold (6) limit (5)
SPVEUATZS   suavest (7) staves (6) paste (5)
GRIMOPADA   paradigm (8) diagram (7) pagoda (6)

$75 + (7 - 3) = 79; (6 + 6) \times 79 = 948$

TRIUMPHED

Round 98
TAGLAVEOC   voltage (7) octave (6) covet (5)
PINDUSORE   prisoned (8) soupier (7) poured (6)
RURCOSATS   curators (8) carrots (7) across (6)

$(2 \times 50) - 6 = 94; 94 \times 4 = 376; 376 + 4 - 3 = 377$

ACCORDION

Round 99
GURESILOG   slogger (7) uglier (6) rogue (5)
XUJOIBKED   jukebox (7) jouked (6) bijou (5)
RFRCIUOLO   couloir (7) frolic (6) curio (5)

$9 \times 9 \times 10 = 810; 25 - (2 \times 7) = 11; 810 + 11 = 821$

TECHNICAL

Round 100
TNDEAELCO   anecdote (8) cleaned (7) decant (6)
EIANRKZSN   snakier (7) sienna (6) inner (5)
ATIDPNYEG   painted (7) taping (6) giant (5)

$7 \times 3 \times 25 = 525; 525 - (10/5) = 523$

PROSECUTE

Round 101
SMRNIEUAR   mariners (8) seminar (7) insure (6)
LTOANDCBE   notable (7) coated (6) blade (5)
ETXCOILVS   costive (7) violet (6) exist (5)

$(4 + 1) \times 50 = 250; 250 + 9 + 8 + 7 = 274$

OFFENDING

Round 102
OEIDNRARN   ordainer (8) randier (7) roared (6)
RCCEUETML   electrum (8) lecture (7) cutler (6)
DSCARNITE   distance (8) stained (7) enacts (6)

$100 - (7 + 6) = 87; 87 \times (5 + 5) = 870; 870 - 2 = 868$

UPSETTING

Round 103
OSLDENWLA   sallowed (8) swollen (7) walled (6)
GOYREHUDN   greyhound (9) hydrogen (8) younger (7)
THORSYEWA   seaworthy (9) wreaths (7) shower (6)

$75 + 8 + 3 = 86; 86 \times 8 = 688; 688 + 6 + 3 = 697$

ORPHANAGE

Round 104

HUGLANSEI	languish (8) sealing (7) single (6)
AVENDUGRE	engraved (8) angered (7) garden (6)
SVAOHRAXE	hoaxers (7) shaver (6) saver (5)

$6 \times (75 + 6) = 486$; $486 - 100 = 386$

LUBRICATE

Round 105

EOTRIANDP	predation (9) ordinate (8) parotid (7)
OFSRECGUT	fructose (8) forgets (7) foster (6)
OSINISNAT	onanists (8) nations (7) insist (6)

$10 \times (7 + 4) = 110$; $(110 - 1) \times 8 = 872$; $872 + 3 = 875$

APPROVING

Round 106

TDJEIURTE	jittered (8) erudite (7) jetted (6)
MSPFIAELH	fishmeal (8) himself (7) flames (6)
BATCLEASM	lambaste (8) calmest (7) stable (6)

$(5 \times 75) + 100 = 475$; $(2 \times 6) - 1 = 11$; $475 - 11 = 464$

EVOLUTION

Round 107

PRNIERSIF	inspirer (8) spinier (7) sniper (6)
GETNGORAB	baronet (7) orange (6) borne (5)
NDRAIUSPE	sprained (8) insured (7) drapes (6)

$(7 \times 8) + 5 = 61$; $61 \times 4 = 244$; $244 + 9 = 253$

MECHANISM

Round 108

RLDOEAVMN	overland (8) removal (7) random (6)
GDBSETOCE	cestode (7) stodge (6) beget (5)
HLDUEAGTR	daughter (8) laughed (7) hurdle (6)

$(3 \times 50) + 10 = 160$; $160 \times 4 = 640$; $640 + 2 = 642$

INCORRECT

Round 109

RPWOETSOE	poorest (7) towers (6) wrote (5)
LYPRUEEIQ	queerly (7) purely (6) equip (5)
SVTDXOIEB	boxiest (7) videos (6) voted (5)

$(8 \times 8) - 6 = 58$; $58 + 75 = 133 \times 7 = 931$

SCAMPERED

Round 110

TZENIGNAE	tzigane (7) negate (6) tinge (5)
YDFAILRAT	frailty (7) ratify (6) tardy (5)
CINCOATRS	narcotics (9) acrostic (8) cartons (7)

$25 - 3 - 2 = 20$; $4 \times 20 = 80$; $(7 \times 100) - 80 = 620$

FORSAKING

Round 111

MTSHOORAD	doormats (8) stardom (7) smooth (6)
GICAETKOD	dockage (7) tacked (6) kited (5)
NIEPSZALR	pralines (8) pilsner (7) lazier (6)

$(8 - 6) + 1 = 3$; $3 \times 7 \times 25 = 525$; $525 + 8 = 533$

RECLINING

Round 112

PFAERDIME	firedamp (8) demirep (7) faired (6)
SCSTOEIRX	exorcists (9) coexists (8) cosiest (7)
LGFOALERT	fellator (8) allegro (7) taller (6)

$75 - (9/9) = 74$; $5 + (10/10) = 6$; $74 \times 6 = 444$

BEDSPREAD

Round 113

BNACOTGES	cognates (8) nosebag (7) agents (6)
AVENRIUGA	vinegar (7) vagina (6) grave (5)
TSPDEAIET	peatiest (8) patties (7) spited (6)

$(8 \times 100) + (3 \times 7) = 821$; $821 - (50/25) = 819$

LANDSCAPE

Round 114

MLTIEOJRS	moister (7) jostle (6) merit (5)
FTSTIEUAM	situate (7) statue (6) fumes (5)
SFIOAMNVU	infamous (8) fauvism (7) fusion (6)

$(10 + 9) \times 50 = 950$; $950 - (6 \times 6) = 914$

GROTESQUE

Round 115

RHYSEAOCB	broaches (8) carboys (7) chores (6)
GRPYOUENG	younger (7) grunge (6) prone (5)
TSRAETMOY	maestro (7) matter (6) smart (5)

$(3 \times 8) + 5 + 2 = 31$; $31 \times 25 = 775$; $775 + 2 = 777$

NERVOUSLY

Round 116

TRFOEILYR	terrify (7) filter (6) rifle (5)
OHEXIDAPE	hexapod (7) hoaxed (6) aphid (5)
EOUZYJTLT	outlet (6) zloty (5) jolt (4)

$6 \times (9 + 1) = 60$; $60 - 2 = 58$; $58 \times (5 \times 2) = 580$

TANTALISE

Round 117

SRTMFOAOK	footmarks (9) formats (7) motors (6)
UAENCLPOS	apolunes (8) capsule (7) places (6)
NLEGGEFEI	negligee (8) feeling (7) niggle (6)

$3 \times (75 - 1) = 222$; $50 - 8 = 42$; $222 + 42 = 264$

PATTERNED

Round 118

TAURHLRBE urethral (8) blather (7) herbal (6)
DESRUMOWG morgues (7) soured (6) drums (5)
IEAHSTNBP thespian (8) baptise (7) habits (6)
$(6 \times 25) - 3 = 147; (5 + 1) \times 147 = 882$
WHIRLPOOL

Round 119

TORIEIFVL vitriol (7) filter (6) olive (5)
RMDEITSAU misrated (8) sidearm (7) muster (6)
BSJYEIECR scribe (6) jeers (5) jibe (4)
$(2 \times 9) + 7 = 25; (4 + 1) \times 6 = 30; 25 \times 30 = 750$
HARMONICA

Round 120

UCEDPIGNN upending (8) penguin (7) gunned (6)
ASCOOGREL aerosol (7) solace (6) gears (5)
SNGOIIRSO origins (7) rising (6) goons (5)
$7 + 7 - 3 = 11; 50 + 11 = 61; 61 \times 4 = 264$
TRANSCEND

Round 121

LMWOEOENT moonlet (7) townee (6) melon (5)
LREEAGSCL cereals (7) caller (6) large (5)
YQLUITAMU quality (7) mutual (6) quail (5)
$(4 \times 25) - (5 + 2) = 93; 3 \times 3 = 9; 93 \times 9 = 837$
IMPORTANT

Round 122

HWXEIADSM admixes (7) shamed (6) waxes (5)
LFMIAURND fluidram (8) maudlin (7) marlin (6)
SYIKLOTEG toylike (7) egoist (6) silky (5)
$8 \times 6 = 48; 48 - (5 - 1) = 44; 44 \times 7 = 308$
RECOUPING

Round 123

NETUSTAFE tetanus (7) fasten (6) tunes (5)
NURISMIVE minivers (8) vermin (6) virus (5)
AISTEDSLN sandiest (8) islands (7) salted (6)
$2 \times 7 \times 50 = 700; (4 \times 8) - 25 = 7; 700 - 7 = 693$
UNFEELING

Round 124

PATURAEVF uprate (6) avert (5) fare (4)
GESIHTEON seething (8) shoeing (7) ingest (6)
AEFGLOPRY leapfrog (8) pergola (7) golfer (6)
$(9 + 8) \times (50 - 4) = 782; 782 + 5 - 3 = 784$
WEALTHIER

Round 125

EFGINORVT	forgiven (8) vertigo (7) roving (6)
ADEILMNST	dismantle (9) manliest (8) stained (7)
CEIINOPRS	precision (9) conspire (8) pincers (7)

$10 \times (10 + 4) = 140;\ 140 + 6 + 2 = 148;\ 148 \times 5 = 740$

GRIMACING

Round 126

GXAHETPNO	pathogen (8) hexagon (7) potage (6)
ENQTUOLPE	eloquent (8) opulent (7) toupee (6)
SAFMEIDHX	famished (8) admixes (7) mashed (6)

$(9 \times 7) - 5 = 58;\ 58 \times 6 = 348;\ 348 - 100 = 248$

SATELLITE

Round 127

AOPLIYELG	pillage (7) goalie (6) loyal (5)
TGYIEDSWA	tideways (8) widgets (7) sweaty (6)
RQPIEGTAU	pratique (8) parquet (7) uprate (6)

$(8 + 2) \times 7 = 70;\ 70 \times 5 = 350;\ 350 - 7 = 343$

SPRAWLING

Round 128

BHEIDOTUR	doubter (7) dither (6) third (5)
PRNDEASOC	endocarps (9) operands (8) respond (7)
NIRULFIEA	airline (7) earful (6) flair (5)

$8 \times (75 - 6) = 552;\ 2 + (4/4) = 3;\ 552 + 3 = 555$

TOUGHENED

Round 129

CRHRWEAOM	charmer (7) marrow (6) chore (5)
NIGYESAVS	essaying (8) sayings (7) vegans (6)
TVLRIOSMA	moralist (8) mistral (7) tailor (6)

$100 + 75 + 50 = 225;\ 225 \times 3 = 675;\ 675 - (4 \times 4) = 659$

CUSTOMARY

Round 130

LTNGEUODL	lounged (7) tongue (6) tolled (6)
PSIOTGAPH	stopgap (7) potash (6) hoist (5)
XRTSNEAOZ	treason (7) extras (6) tenor (5)

$(8 \times 3) + 1 = 25;\ 25 \times 25 = 625;\ 625 - (4 - 1) = 622$

RADIATION

Round 131

FCLDIOEVR	frivoled (8) divorce (7) folder (6)
HRBATIATE	habitat (7) batter (6) heart (5)
TGSBIAEJL	giblets (7) ligate (6) jails (5)

$6 + (100/25) = 10;\ 75 + 9 = 84;\ 84 \times 10 = 840$

ENTHUSING

Round 132

DNPUEIKTL   tinkled (7) pinked (6) unlit (5)

DPEOHSEGO   sheepdog (8) hooped (6) hoods (5)

RSWEGOEKN   knowers (7) worsen (6) weeks (5)

$(9 \times 10) - 10 = 80$; $(80 + 1) \times 9 = 729$; $729 - 100 = 629$

LIMITLESS

Round 133

CXOALURNO   coronal (7) racoon (6) coral (5)

CSEOTHEMF   fetches (7) themes (6) comet (5)

STAXUALDR   austral (7) adults (6) darts (5)

$9 \times 9 \times 3 \times 3 = 729$

COSSETING

Round 134

DTEIPSENO   pentodes (8) pointed (7) stoned (6)

WTMEAIRDS   readmits (8) wartime (7) mister (6)

STIEUKWOS   ketosis (7) tissue (6) tusks (5)

$(6 + 3) \times (100 - 10) = 810$; $810 - (7 + 2) = 805$

QUIESCENT

Round 135

OLCXSEAOV   alcoves (7) coaxes (6) slave (5)

MTCNIEOAI   amniotic (8) aconite (6) inmate (6)

GERINDERA   grenadier (9) gardener (8) reading (7)

$(6 \times 25) + 3 = 153$; $153 \times 2 = 306$; $306 + 5 = 311$

DISCOLOUR

Round 136

NHTEIJREA   herniate (8) hairnet (7) retina (6)

CLOETDIPE   piloted (7) police (6) optic (5)

SANRELNSA   arsenals (8) anneals (7) learns (6)

$(6 \times 25) + 50 = 200$; $(200 + 6) \times 4 = 824$; $824 - 4 = 820$

ENDORSING

Round 137

NESOLCGEZ   lozenges (8) enclose (7) clones (6)

WOITHRSEE   otherwise (9) theorise (8) withers (7)

KAOBDHITI   adhibit (7) aikido (6) habit (5)

$100 + 10 + 7 = 117$; $(8/2) \times 117 = 468$

SUBSCRIBE

Round 138

MATYVOLNE   novelty (7) yeoman (6) ovate (5)

ATGRAEKXU   gateaux (7) karate (6) grate (5)

RANEUHPET   urethane (8) panther (7) uprate (6)

$(8 - 6) \times 75 = 150$; $150 + 5 + 4 = 159$; $159 \times 5 = 795$

INSINCERE

Round 139

NISDANVEH   vanished (8) invades (7) sienna (6)
ATHERTONS   rheostat (8) shatter (7) hornet (6)
XIMENESDO   demonise (8) indexes (7) onside (6)

$(9 + 2) \times 9 = 99; 99 \times 6 = 594; 594 - 8 = 586$

SCREWBALL

Round 140

GUTTAPOER   tutorage (8) garotte (7) putter (6)
IMUVNECAR   manicure (8) numeric (7) craven (6)
TUEQALSIY   equality (8) tequila (7) quails (6)

$(7 + 5) \times (6 + 1) = 84; (84 \times 10) + 2 = 842$

SPAGHETTI

Round 141

NODIFAETS   sedation (8) instead (7) fasten (6)
ASCEDACHD   cascaded (8) saccade (7) cashed (6)
DSKIEULFT   flukiest (8) dilutes (7) tusked (6)

$(9 + 2) \times (5 - 2) = 33; 75 + 33 = 108; 108 \times 8 = 864$

DESTROYED

Round 142

RDGOEVARP   prograde (8) vapored (7) groped (6)
DMSMEIASL   dilemmas (8) mislead (7) slides (6)
PDTIEANTL   pantiled (8) planted (7) planet (6)

$100 - (8 + 4) = 88; 88 \times 6 = 528; 528 - (1 + 1) = 526$

BATTERING

Round 143

LRGOEOSNC   consoler (8) cologne (7) longer (6)
SNWOIATPU   opuntias (8) outspan (7) patios (6)
RYRAIABLS   library (7) salary (6) array (5)

$4 \times 3 \times 3 = 36; (36 + 1) \times 25 = 925; 925 - 2 = 923$

HEARTENED

Round 144

LXPEAEFHM   example (7) female (6) expel (5)
RCTMAIEGD   grimaced (8) ragtime (7) midget (6)
TNLEAESTK   anklets (7) kettle (6) steak (5)

$8 \times 2 \times 2 = 32; 32 \times 25 = 800; 800 - (10 + 9) = 781$

NUMBERING

Round 145

BGFAOIERT   frigate (7) boater (6) brief (5)
SPOIGMEOB   boogies (7) impose (6) poise (5)
FIUIGLSET   uglifies (8) utilise (7) stifle (6)

$3 \times 75 = 225; 225 - 5 - 4 - 1 = 215; 215 \times 4 = 860$

DEVASTATE

Round 146

SUETYOISL   lousiest (8) solutes (7) tissue (6)
QIUAERFGH   aquifer (7) figure (6) quire (5)
URDBISLEG   builders (8) gerbils (7) guilds (6)
$(7 + 2) \times 50 = 450$; $450 + 8 = 458$; $458 \times (5 - 3) = 916$
TRIBUTARY

Round 147

NDEAMLICE   limeade (7) menace (6) denim (5)
DTINOMANE   nominated (9) dominate (8) domaine (7)
LASTELITE   satellite (9) tallest (7) titles (6)
$(4 \times 25) - 7 = 93$; $93 \times (4 + 1) = 465$
GROUNDING

Round 148

AEMPROSTU   mousetrap (9) tempuras (8) pasture (7)
TEINDLQUO   outlined (8) quoined (7) dilute (6)
YLDOTRAZI   adroitly (8) tardily (7) lizard (6)
$(8 \times 5) = 40$; $40 \times (7 + 1) = 320$; $320 + 9 = 329$
TURNTABLE

Round 149

RAIREBLYZ   bizarrely (9) library (7) lazier (6)
UPTHENOSE   penthouse (9) potheens (8) enthuse (7)
RSTOIDEWU   wordiest (8) tedious (7) duster (6)
$(6 + 4) \times 75 = 750$; $750 + 100 = 850$; $850 - (3/3) = 849$
MODELLING

Round 150

PORACETOV   overcoat (8) overact (7) vector (6)
ZDPIOMTEH   ethmoid (7) method (6) hoped (5)
NLXOASTOI   oxtails (7) lotion (6) stool (5)
$(3 \times 5) + 10 = 25$; $25 \times 25 = 625$; $625 + 6 - 7 = 624$
CULMINATE

Round 151

LRMEOTNIV   violent (7) motive (6) lemon (5)
TANOVUGTE   tutenag (7) nougat (6) vaunt (5)
SAENTMING   steaming (8) teasing (7) magnet (6)
$8 \times 9 = 72$; $72 \times (8 + 1) = 648$; $648 + 2 = 650$
SURCHARGE

Round 152

XATGALHEW   wealth (6) algae (5) axle (4)
OISNVADEH   vanished (8) invades (7) onside (6)
LAMTEYTIS   steamily (8) stately (7) metals (6)
$(3 \times 6) \times (50 + 5) = 990$; $990 - (9 - 7) = 988$
INTERVIEW

Round 153

NTZOAIPRE   patronize (9) atropine (8) painter (7)
BOJEDGANA   bandage (7) agenda (6) banjo (5)
ACEEHILVR   chevalier (9) acheiver (8) archive (7)

$5 + 3 + 1 = 9; 9 \times (75 - 1) = 666$

DISCOVERY

Round 154

ABEIJNORW   rainbow (7) joiner (6) brown (5)
ACEFLONRY   falconry (8) corneal (7) crayon (6)
STEUPEALC   speculate (9) epaulets (8) capsule (7)

$6 + 3 = 18 \times 50 = 900; 5 + 1 = 6 \times 4 = 24; 900 - 24 = 876$

PURCHASED

Round 155

OOTHPASTE   osteopath (9) potatoes (8) teapots (7)
EHIOPSURV   pushover (8) soupier (7) hovers (6)
CEEEGINRT   energetic (9) erecting (8) integer (7)

$(9 \times 2) \times (50 - 1) = 882; 882 - 7 = 875$

BLUEPRINT

Round 156

ADEILMTTU   mutilated (9) altitude (8) mutated (7)
HAGNIBEDE   beheading (9) bighead (7) gained (6)
LEDSARBOU   laboured (8) roulade (7) blades (6)

$(7 + 6) \times 10 = 130; (130 + 1) \times (2 \times 2) = 524$

PERSPIRED

Round 157

MNOTPLREA   patrolmen (9) temporal (8) trample (7)
DALLISEWK   sidewalk (8) skilled (7) ladies (6)
ZERTILSEI   sterilize (9) zestier (7) litres (6)

$8 + 6 + 1 = 15; (8 \times 25) - 15 = 185; 185 \times 3 = 555$

FROLICKED

Round 158

LETOMGIRO   gloomier (8) legroom (7) loiter (6)
PNIELDCKU   unpicked (8) pickled (7) licked (6)
HLOPESTOS   potholes (8) topless (7) hostel (6)

$(75 + 9) \times 10 = 840; 840 - (5 + 2) = 833$

LEGENDARY

Round 159

GRVINYCEA   vinegary (8) craving (7) grainy (6)
TLPAEOYNR   ornately (8) penalty (7) teapoy (6)
TYAUELSHV   suavely (7) sleuth (6) lusty (5)

$(5 + 4) \times (100 - 7) = 837; 837 + 6 + 6 = 849$

DOWNRIGHT

Round 160

JENIOSGLS   jingles (7) losing (6) gloss (5)
CCEENDORS   crescendo (9) concedes (8) endorse (7)
ALIMROSTU   simulator (9) altruism (8) mortals (7)

100/4 = 25; 25 x 25 = 625; 625 + 50 + 1 = 676

WITHERING

Answers to Games

Game 1 (Scott Mearns)
ROADMEN
BANISH
PRIMATES

570 (100 − 4 x 6 − 3 − 3)

WIZARD
STEAMING
CANTERED

161 (75/25 − 2 + 100 + 50 + 10)

PREPARING

Game 2 (Allan Saldanha)
LIAISON
NEATLY
POTENT

581 (9 − 3 = 6 x 100 − 9 − 10)

REACTING
BUTTON
GAYNESS

567 (10 + 10 x 25 + 8 x 9 − 5)

No answer offered (POLLUTION)

Game 3 (Liz Barber)
BOASTED
FLAIRS
TIDDLY

134 (8 − 5 x 50 − 10 − 7 + 1)

PIOUS
REPLIED
ADROIT

162 (5 + 1 x 25 + 8 + 4)

DISPORTED

Game 4 (Harvey Freeman)
NATURIZES (disallowed)
ANGELIC
CONKED

726 (5 x 2 x 10 x 7 + 1 + 25)

MOIETY
SAFARI
HEEDING

784 (disallowed – mistake)

INSOLENCE

Game 5 (Kate Ogilvie)
FANCIER
MOGULS
DREAMS

454 (75 x 6 + 8/2)

SOAKED
AMENDING
OUTCRY

NOTHING DECLARED

REWRITING

Game 6 (David Elias)
TOASTED
EXACTIONS
MEAGRELY

520 (4 + 3 x 75 + 3 + 50/25)

BATCHES
LONLIER (disallowed)
HOARD

509 (25 x 2 + 1 x 7 + 3 – 1)

SHARKSKIN

Game 7 (Wayne Kelly)
REGULATE
SOILED
PARISH

533 (7 x 3 x 25 + 9 – 1)

BOLDEST
SCREAMS
SPINNER

920 (100 + 1 x 9 + 6 + 5)

SCRUFFIER

Game 8 (Ray McPhie)

FAINTED
MALINGER
STANDS

449 (100 + 10 x 4 + 7 + 2)

BEAMERS
ASCEND
UMPIRE

732 (7 x 4 + 1 = 29 x 25 + 9 – 2)

MONOLOGUE

Game 9 (David Acton)

SPEARING
OESTRUM
WILTED

167 (4 x 25 + 10 x 6 + 7)

SODOMY
FIERCEST
DENIAL

384 (25 x 7 + 2 + 2)

UNSMILING

Game 10 (Wayne Summers)

SAVES
MALTIER
HUNTER

100 (10 x 10)

PONDER
SCREWING
DREAMING

743 (6 x 5 x 25 + 8 + 2 – 3)

No answer offered (EMULATING)